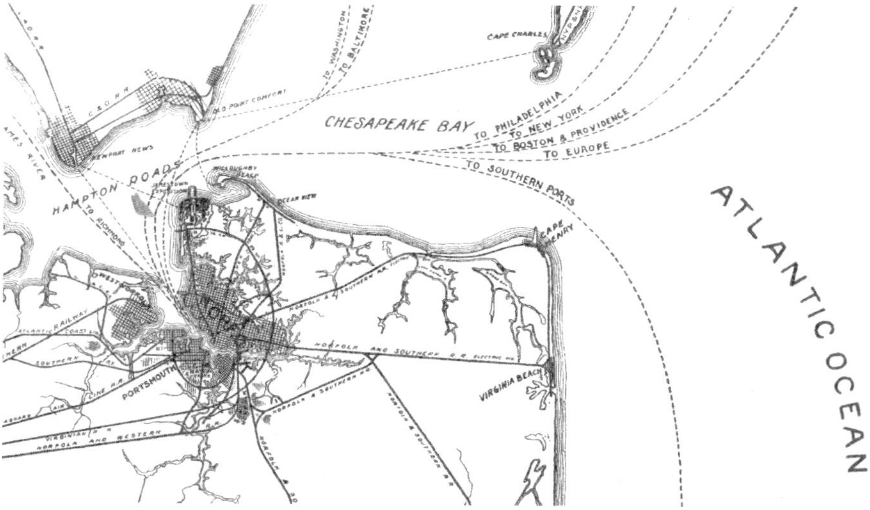

Map of Norfolk from a 1914 promotional booklet published by the Norfolk Industrial Commission. *Bangor Public Library.*

On This Day In NORFOLK VIRGINIA HISTORY

SARAH DOWNING

THE History PRESS

Published by The History Press
Charleston, SC 29403
www.historypress.net

Front cover, top left: Norfolk at night. *Wikimedia Commons*; *left, second from bottom*: *Rubber Duck* sculpture. *Wikimedia Commons*.

First published 2015

Manufactured in the United States

ISBN 978.1.62619.703.9

Library of Congress Control Number: 2015938643

CONTENTS

ACKNOWLEDGEMENTS

Compiling a book takes lots of energy, patience, time and help. I would like to thank the following people for their generosity:

Eddie Woodward, archives coordinator, Norfolk Public Library

Kelly Welsh, public relations specialist, Norfolk Botanical Garden

Mel Frizzell, special collections specialist, Special Collections and University Archives, Perry Library, Old Dominion University

James Zobel, MacArthur Memorial

Sherrie Barnes, Amanda Albarty and Tiffany Bryant, Dare County Library

Brandon W. Stilley, Bryna Coonin, David Hilse and Matt Reynolds, Joyner Library, East Carolina University

J. Banks Smither, The History Press, my kind, patient, diplomatic and insightful editor

Jane Wills, Virginia Tech Digital Collections

Defense Video and Imagery Distribution System

Youlanda Logan, Jimmy Carter Library and Museum

I would especially like to thank James B. Currie of Norfolk, who allowed me to use his modern-day color photographs of the city that really speak to the soul of Norfolk. I am deeply grateful that his images are included. They add so much.

Also, special thanks to Connie Perkins, who is the best proofreader and friend a gal can have!

INTRODUCTION

In 1680, Norfolk, Virginia, was established several miles from Cape Henry at the mouth of the Chesapeake Bay. Its nearness to navigable waterways helped Norfolk develop. Land was purchased, and homes and businesses were built. In 1736, the settlement was elevated in status to become a borough. Warehouses along the waterfront were filled with tobacco, cotton and lumber from the Old Dominion and neighboring North Carolina for shipment to Europe or the West Indies.

During the American Revolution, four British ships ushered in 1776 when they "celebrated" the New Year by shelling the city on January 1 in the early pre-dawn hours. Local Patriots burned the city, lest it fall to British hands. Loyalist citizens and others fled to the country to escape the melee.

Tragedy and pestilence struck Norfolk and Portsmouth in 1855 when an outbreak of yellow fever overtook the port cities. It was believed the disease sailed into Hampton Roads that summer, and it quickly spread. Dozens of people died each day. Panic ensued, and many left town, while residents in neighboring towns waited and prayed. The outbreak diminished in the autumn following a hard frost.

Norfolk witnessed much activity during the American Civil War. The city became part of the Confederacy when Virginia seceded from the Union in the spring of 1861. President Lincoln bolstered manpower at the federally controlled Fort Monroe across Hampton Roads. Additional federal property, the Gosport Naval Shipyard at Portsmouth, was burned by members of the Union navy who feared ships and ordnance would fall into Confederate hands.

One of the vessels scuttled at the navy yard, the USS *Merrimack*, was refurbished and upgraded with iron siding to become what was described as a battering ram that menaced the U.S. blockading fleet. Renamed the CSS

Virginia, it battled to a draw with the Union ship *Monitor* on March 9, 1862, after laying waste to the wooden frigate USS *Cumberland* the day before.

By the close of the nineteenth century, Norfolk was a bustling port and boasted of its access to the ocean and freedom from ice that plagued harbors farther to the north. Cotton, oysters, peanuts, coal and lumber were the city's leading exports. Promotional literature of the time made note of Norfolk's modern infrastructure, which included electric lights, a large trolley system and a functioning sewer system based on the Waring plan. Two hospitals, numerous churches and places of worship representing many religious groups and a public library were institutions that defined Norfolk as a civilized city.

The new century brought the spotlight to Pine Beach, on the outskirts of the city. It was the scene of the much-publicized Jamestown Exposition, a multi-month fair created to commemorate the founding of the first permanent English settlement in America at Jamestown, just up the James River from Norfolk. The site of the Exposition was chosen because it offered more accommodations, train access and easier accessibility via boat than Jamestown, the actual settlement of the 1607 colony.

The site of the Jamestown Exposition was considered a prime spot for a naval base, and after the United States entered World War I, the property was purchased by the federal government. The following year, thirty-four thousand enlisted personnel were stationed at Naval Operating Base (NOB). Additional land was purchased or created by dredging, which allowed the base to expand. Buildings were constructed, runways paved and piers built to allow for the dockage of large ships.

The onslaught of World War II and the rise of Norfolk's defense industry brought thousands to its shores and created a need for additional housing, roads and public transportation. The city's population grew by almost 50 percent between 1940 and 1950.

Following the war, Norfolk became the first city in America to take advantage of the federal Housing Act of 1949 and began a massive urban renewal project, removing slums and constructing new houses and municipal buildings. The changing face of the city included the introduction of many new structures that would be identified with a new Norfolk.

Walter P. Chrysler moved his art collection to the city, and the former Norfolk Museum of Arts and Sciences became the Chrysler Museum. During the 1970s, two downtown venues, Scope and Chrysler Hall, began hosting concerts and sporting events. By the 1980s, architect James Rouse put his mark on the downtown waterfront with the addition of Waterside. Town Point Park began to host events and festivals with a view of the Elizabeth River.

In the past twenty-five years, Nauticus, Harbor Park, the MacArthur Center and the USS *Wisconsin* have become downtown fixtures. The Norfolk Naval Base is the world's largest, and the city is one of the nation's busiest ports. But Norfolk is not just a city of buildings and industry; it is a city of diverse people. Norfolk is home to close to 250,000 residents who live in the city's many vibrant neighborhoods that reflect different periods of Norfolk's history.

With over three hundred years of history from which to draw, this compilation of vignettes was assembled as an act of love and respect to honor my hometown by the sea.

JANUARY

January 1

1776—Brits Burn City

British forces under the command of Virginia governor Lord Dunmore bombarded Norfolk from a number of ships anchored in Hampton Roads Harbor. Norfolk was predominately loyal to Great Britain. American Patriots, who did not want the city to leave any provisions to their invaders, laid the town to waste, ensuring that no British soldiers would be housed there. After the destruction, only the walls of the Borough Church (now known as St. Paul's Episcopal) were left standing. The city's ideal location made it resilient, and citizens returned so that Norfolk was America's eighth most populous city in 1800.

January 2

2008—City Aims to Host MEAC Tourneys

City officials announced plans to vie for the opportunity to host the 2009 Mid-Eastern Athletic Conference (MEAC) men's and women's basketball tournaments held for three years in Raleigh. North Carolina's capital city did not renew its contract for the upcoming year. Norfolk hosted MEAC tournaments from 1991 to 1993 and again in 1997, and while the 2009–2013 tournaments were awarded to Winston-Salem, North Carolina, the MEAC returned to the Mermaid City in 2013–2015. Norfolk State University plays in the MEAC league, which is composed of teams from historically black colleges and universities.

January 3

1858—Hoop Skirt Saves Woman from Drowning

While attempting to board the steamer *Jamestown*, Jane Johnson, a woman of color, fell into the Elizabeth River. She happened to remain buoyant due to her "Sunday hoop skeart," which kept her head above water until "dat dare gemman flung me de line, which I cotch and hilt on to 'tell dey pulled me on da land." It was reported that although Jane was scared by the experience, she was long on the praise of her hoop skirt. The "gemmen" who threw Jane the line was a Mr. Roberts, second mate on the *Jamestown.*

January 4

2005—City Council Abolishes Vehicle Decals

The Norfolk City Council voted unanimously to do away with the three-inch by three-inch decals required to be displayed on the windshields of cars and small trucks. Although the annual sticker would become a thing of the past, the twenty-six-dollar fee would still be passed along to city vehicle owners via property taxes. City treasurer Thomas Moss was ecstatic and told council members that the taxpayers would be thankful for the move. Virginia Beach had also done away with city vehicle stickers, and Portsmouth, Chesapeake and Suffolk followed suit soon after Norfolk abandoned its sticker system.

January 5

1940—Norfolk Merchandise Broker Executed in Richmond

James Clifton Abdell, who was convicted for the May 1938 murder of his wife, Audrey, was put to death by electrocution at the Virginia State Penitentiary. Abdell was accused of beating his spouse unconscious and then turning on the gas jets and leaving her to die in their Norfolk apartment. Following the execution, Abdell's body was taken via hearse back to Norfolk for burial.

January 6

1958—Navy Plane Crashes at Ocean View

A navy patrol plane crashed at Ocean View after its engines failed. Four of the Mercator aircraft's crew of twelve perished in the incident, and three people on the ground were injured when the plane struck two vehicles and six bay-front cottages. The pilot reported that he was in position to land at the Norfolk Naval Air Station when an engine lost power. He attempted to land the airplane at sea to avoid injury but was unable to do so.

January 7

1995—Lawrence and Southall Exchange Vows

Comedian Martin Lawrence wed Tidewater native and beauty queen Patricia Southall in a ceremony at Norfolk's Waterside Marriott Hotel. Among the six hundred guests were comedians Eddie Murphy and Will Smith and boxer Sweet Pea Whitaker. Outside, hundreds more were gathered, hoping for a peek at the festivities. Southall, Miss Virginia 1992 and first runner-up to Miss USA 1994, had eighteen bridesmaids in the ceremony. The ladies wore cream-colored gowns accentuated with pearls and accessorized with formal full-length gloves. The couple had one child together but separated and divorced within two years.

January 8

1970—Funding for Ports Prompts Governor's Visit

Members of the Norfolk Port and Industrial Authority informed state senator Edward L. Breeden Jr., chairman of the Virginia Ports Study Commission, that immediate funding needs of the port were just as important as long-range planning. Following the luncheon where the information was shared, Breedan arranged for Virginia governor Mills E. Godwin Jr. to fly in the following day and address authorities. Godwin spoke to a closed session in the Port Room at Norfolk International Airport. A report issued by the study commission recommended creating a long-range plan for a unified ports system.

January 9

1924—"The Lady From Norfolk" One of Two Female Legislators

Norfolkian Sarah Lee Fain and Buchanan County's Helen Timmons Henderson became the first two women to serve in the Virginia House of Delegates. Their election came after the 1920 ratification of the Nineteenth Amendment to the U.S. Constitution, which gave women the right to vote. Fain was encouraged to run for public office after influencing Norfolk women to help reelect Virginia governor Claude A. Swanson. Fain proved popular with her constituents and heartily defeated her opponent in the 1925 election and ran unopposed in 1927. She ran unsuccessfully for the U.S. House of Representatives in 1929 and later moved to Washington, D.C., where she held a number of federal government positions, including director of the U.S. Information Service.

January 10

1970—Retired Editor Dies in City

Lenoir Chambers, former editor of the *Virginian-Pilot* newspaper, died at Norfolk General Hospital. During his newspaper career, which spanned forty-one years, he earned recognition for his disapproval of the state's policy of massive resistance, Virginia's method of fighting school desegregation. Chambers won a Pulitzer Prize for his editorial writing in the *Pilot* for a series of pieces in opposition to school closings and organized efforts against school integration. His biography of General Thomas J. "Stonewall" Jackson was also nominated for a Pulitzer Prize.

January 11

1878—Artist of Note Found Dead in Studio

E. Boneau De St. Marcel, a Polish-born portrait painter, was found dead in his Main Street studio. The artist had been in poor health and without any real means of support other than caring friends. His cause of death was determined to be lung congestion. In his native country, De St. Marcel was known as Count Edward Jablonski and, along with thirteen others of similar rank, had been banished from his homeland by an imperial decree, or ukase. A Russian ship brought him to New York City in 1837. De St. Marcel settled in Norfolk after one of his traveling paintings burned when it was on display in Mechanics Hall.

January 12

1942—Streetcar Drivers Sought

An advertisement run by the Virginia Electric and Power Company (VEPCO) appeared in a Danville, Virginia newspaper on this day to recruit bus drivers and streetcar operators for routes in Norfolk and Portsmouth. Wartime conditions created an urgent need to improve and increase public transportation for defense workers and sailors. VEPCO was interested in hiring married folks between the ages of twenty-one and forty between five foot six and six foot one who could pass both physical and mental tests.

January 13

1966—Macarthur Murals Presented to City

Six murals depicting various scenes of the life of General Douglas MacArthur were given to the city. The paintings, a gift of the Edwin Austin Abbey Memorial

Mural on display at the MacArthur Memorial depicting scenes from the life of General Douglas MacArthur. *Courtesy MacArthur Memorial Archives and Library.*

Fund of the National Academy of Design, were commissioned for $30,000 and created by Larchmont, New York artist Alton Tobey. On hand for the ceremony was Jean Marie Faircloth MacArthur, widow of the esteemed general, who is buried in Norfolk. She was reported as saying, "They are wonderful," referring to the murals.

January 14

1933—Norfolk Girl Attempts Suicide in New York

A tragedy took place when nineteen-year-old Norfolkian Sally Barron attempted to take her own life by severing a blood vessel in her elbow using a pair of scissors. Ambulance surgeons treated her at the scene. Miss Barron had been in New York for two weeks and had grown despondent about her inability to find work in the Big Apple. She was the daughter of James S. Barron, a Norfolk attorney and former state senator.

January 15

1895—Bolt Gives Way, Sends Horse Trader Tumbling

An unfortunate incident occurred when Mr. H.H. Wise received a severe laceration and bruises on his face after a bolt on the buggy in which he was riding broke and sent him toppling over the spatter board. Wise, a horse trader known about town, was traveling with Mr. J.H. Robinson of Edenton, North Carolina, when the calamitous episode took place. Dr. Hunter treated Wise, who was described as "a very heavy man."

January 16

2003—Officer Killed in the Line of Duty

While interviewing a potential gunman following a barroom shooting, Sheila Herring-Patrick, a thirty-nine-year-old Norfolk police officer, was fatally wounded by the suspect and died later at Norfolk General Sentara Hospital. Other officers at the scene killed the gunman. The incident took place around 1:45 a.m. at Champion's Sports Bar on Brambleton Avenue.

Herring-Patrick, who began her law enforcement career in Detroit, was the first female police officer to lose her life in the line of duty in Norfolk. She had been with the NPD for less than a year before the fatal incident.

January 17

1950—"Big Mo" Runs Aground

The battleship USS *Missouri*, the only active U.S. battleship, ran aground in shallow water near Thimble Shoals on its way to Guantanamo Bay, Cuba. Twelve tugs were sent to nudge the great ship from the bar on which it was stuck but were unable to accomplish the task, and it was decided to wait for a turn in the tide. After two weeks, and after a special channel was dredged alongside "Mighty Mo," the ship was freed by the use of a dozen tugboats and favorable tides that were raised by the chop of a brisk northeast breeze that whipped waves to four and five feet.

January 18

1857—Blizzard of '57 Strikes City

Norfolk was one of many East Coast cities to be buried under a foot of snow during what would be known as the Blizzard of 1857, also called the "Cold Storm." Following this snowfall, a second blast of frigid air arrived days later, and temperatures plummeted below zero. It was so cold during this period that the Elizabeth River froze, and people walked freely between Norfolk and Portsmouth over the ice. In fact, the entire Chesapeake Bay and its tributaries were frozen solid.

January 19

1900—Washington Post Reports on Lamb's Request

The *Washington Post* reported that Colonel William Lamb appeared before the lighthouse board and presented a request signed by businessmen, leading citizens and transportation representatives suggesting that navigational lights be placed in Hampton Roads Channel leading to the harbor at Norfolk.

The installation would allow ships wanting to load coal to do so day or night. Members of the board told Lamb they would recommend a $40,000 appropriation for this improvement to navigation.

January 20

1898—Medical Association Formed

Ninety-nine doctors from the Tidewater region of Virginia and eastern North Carolina met in the city to form the Seaboard Medical Association. At its organizational session, it was decided that the group would assemble semi-annually in January and July and that the meetings would be held in Norfolk (or within thirty miles of the city) but would also alternate to various North Carolina cities. Membership was limited to graduates of bona fide medical schools. Dr. Southgate Leigh presented a talk about his recent work with X-rays, after which he entertained the group at his stately Granby Street home for a late-night banquet. Oysters, chicken croquettes, apple toddies and champagne were enjoyed by the guests prior to coffee and cigars.

January 21

1898—Ohio Governor Tours City

While spending a few days at Old Point Comfort with his wife, son and daughter-in-law, Ohio governor Asa S. Bushnell took a morning to see the sights of Norfolk. On his itinerary was St. Paul's Church and the navy yard. The governor traveled incognito and, in so doing, did not receive any military honors normally bestowed on someone of his stature. It was reported, however, that he was recognized while boarding a steamer to return to the peninsula. Bushnell and family were staying at the Chamberlain Hotel and came to Virginia for health reasons.

January 22

1866—Newspaper Tells of Transitional Times in City

This day's edition of the *Norfolk Post* included a letter signed by a number of black pastors speaking on behalf of the "respectful and intelegent coloud citizens of Norfolk" [*sic*] that denounced the actions of an inferior class of blacks. They were described as paupers, vagabonds, highway robbers and murderers who had followed the army from Baltimore, Washington and Petersburg. The letter urged city leaders to grant Negroes citizenship and the right to testify in court. Alongside the aforementioned article was another telling of the increase in nighttime violence befalling those on the streets at a late hour. Thugging or garroting by ruffians and thieves of both races had become a public outrage that called for a change in the "system of police" to keep up with "the great change in the social condition of our people."

January 23

1963—Larchmont Man Recognized for Patriotism

After seven years of proudly flying an American flag at his home at the corner of Hampton Boulevard and Bolling Avenue, Mr. Clayton Wiggs was recognized by sailors from the aircraft carrier *Randolph*. They presented Wiggs, a retired businessman, with a flag that had been flown aboard the ship. Wiggs's flag was seen by thousands of people who traversed the busy intersection, including students at Larchmont Elementary School and Old Dominion College. A navy bugler and a four-man color guard were on hand to present the flag to Wiggs.

January 24

1853—Norwegian-Born Violinist Entertains at Mechanic's Hall

Ole Bull, a noted Scandinavian violinist, played the first of two concerts in the city to enthusiastic and appreciative crowds. Bull, who began playing violin as a child, was accompanied by eight-year-old Spanish-born soprano Adelina Patti, described as a "musical wonder," and her sister Amalia

Norwegian violinist Ole Bull played to a packed house in Norfolk. *Brady-Handy Collection, Library of Congress.*

Patti Strakosch. The venue was said to be "crowded to its fullest capacity." Following his two concerts, the eccentric musician traveled by boat to Baltimore for another performance.

January 25

1877—German Club Fêtes Russians

Grand Duke Alexis and members of the Russian royal family were on an extended visit to Norfolk, and on this evening, the Norfolk German Club arranged a complimentary German, a type of cotillion dance popular at the time. The dance was attended by some of the royals as well as officers of the frigate *Swetlana*, a vessel of the Royal Imperial Navy. The hall where the ball was held was decorated with flags of the United States and Russia and was the scene of unusual splendor and brilliancy. Women were dressed in the finest silks and adorned with gold and diamonds. Refreshments were served close to midnight, and the affair continued until the early morning hours.

January 26

1996—Macarthur Mall Groundbreaking Held on General's Birthday

Seven hundred people were on hand for the groundbreaking of the MacArthur Center, a $300 million, twenty-acre shopping mall. Dillards and Nordstrom would be two of the three anchors in the new facility that would house one hundred specialty shops. It was hoped that MacArthur Center might lure thirty thousand shoppers downtown each day. The opening ceremonies included a cluster of five stars (which represented General MacArthur) rising from a wooden replica cake that was festooned with fireworks and confetti. The mall was not without its detractors, who pointed to other attractions, such as Nauticus and Waterside, that were also vying for their share of visitors' dollars.

January 27

1983—Shoplifter Convicted of Second Charge

A twenty-four-year-old mother of three was found guilty of not only of concealing merchandise but also of contributing to the delinquency of a minor. The woman was with her four-year-old daughter when an employee at a department store overheard the mother encourage her daughter to sneak a five-dollar pair of earrings in her pocket. The woman pled guilty to contributing to the delinquency of a minor charge and was fined, but she appealed the conviction on the concealment charge.

January 28

1900—Need for Harbor Lights Stressed Following Barge Collision

While leaving its portage, the Old Dominion steamer *Princess Anne* ran into the large coal barge *Brooklyn,* which was moored in the channel off Lambert's Point. The steamer continued on its voyage to New York, but the barge, which suffered from a great gash, sank. The incident followed on the heels of the grounding of the vessel *Jamestown,* and both accidents drew attention to the need for lighted buoys in Norfolk Harbor.

January 29

1963—Council Cracks Down on Thumbing Rides

City council voted to ban the practice of hitchhiking after receiving several complaints of young people aggressively trying to pick up rides, even at times tapping on car windows. Wards Corner and other corners along Granby Street were named as the key points for kids looking for a lift. A fifty-dollar fine would be imposed on anyone violating the new ordinance, which allowed for asking acquaintances for rides and hitchhiking in times of emergency. The law would go into effect on March 1.

January 30

1974—Basketball Stars Meet at Scope

The American Basketball Association (ABA) held its seventh annual All-Star Game at Norfolk's Scope Arena, one of the home courts of the Virginia Squires. The teams were divided as East versus West. The ABA, known for its red, white and blue basketball, consisted of teams such as the New

Jersey Nets, Indiana Pacers and Spirits of St. Louis. At the final buzzer, the East topped the West 128–112. Atis Gilmore of the Kentucky Colonels was named the game's most valuable player.

January 31

2005—Zebra and Lion Have Happenstance Encounter

Over at the Virginia Zoo, Zeke the Zebra—a Grant's zebra, to be specific—somehow made his way out of his exhibit enclosure and found his way to the lion area, where he met up with Kalisa, resident lioness. When zoo staff found the two together, the four-year-old zebra and six-year-old lion were catawampus from each other, each in a corner. Zeke was reported as sporting some scratch marks, while Kalisa appeared wet and muddy. Zoo director Lewis Greene was surprised at Zeke's errant meandering, saying, "What enticed him to go over there, we have no idea."

FEBRUARY

February 1

1953—Tugboat Crews Strike

The third tugboat strike in as many years stalled the commercial shipping of goods. The striking workers wanted a 10 percent pay increase, three additional holidays and additional pay for work on Sundays and between midnight and 6:30 a.m. Simultaneous strikes took place in New York and Philadelphia.

February 2

1959—Schools Begin to Integrate

A group of black students, dubbed the Norfolk Seventeen, attended classes at city high schools and junior high schools that, up until that time, were all white. Norfolk's schools had been closed for five months in an attempt to delay the Supreme Court's *Brown vs. Board of Education* decision. While well over one hundred black students applied to enter the white schools, testing and interviews narrowed the group to seventeen students who received organized and rigorous coaching on how to handle racial conflicts, their role as "agents of social change" and how to succeed academically. Not only did the youngsters experience name-calling and tension, but they were also often isolated in the school setting. Their ability to persevere paved the road for others.

February 3

1961—Department Stores Allow Black Diners

Three Norfolk department stores followed a trend taking place in other southern cities such as Richmond and Nashville, Tennessee, and opened their dining rooms to black customers. Rices, Smith and Welton and Ames and Brownley were the department stores that changed their policies. A statement was released stating, "We believe this action to be in the best interest of the entire community in view that similar action has taken place in other southern cities," Lunch counters in five-and-dime stores were already integrated.

February 4

1960—Norfolk Named All-American City

Norfolk was one of eleven cities awarded the title of All-American City by the National Municipal League and *Look* magazine. Mayor Duckworth was proud as he raised a flag with the prestigious moniker over city hall for all to see and to stir a sense of community pride. At a celebratory luncheon held later, *Look*'s publisher, Vernon C. Myers, in his address to the crowd, described Norfolk as a city "with a bright new character." The award came following a major downtown slum removal and urban renewal project.

February 5

1920—Willoughby Beach Severed from Mainland

Following a fierce two-day winter gale, a breach was made across Willoughby Spit, cutting the tip of that peninsula off from Ocean View and the rest of the city. Both beach resorts suffered damage in the storm. Cottages had their foundations undermined by the above-normal tides. Bulkheads and pilings were washed away in the high water. Initial estimates put the damage at $750,000. Floods in the downtown area were reported to be up to three feet higher than normal. Temporary bridges were constructed to allow pedestrian traffic about the city.

February 6

1821—Flour Storage Options Increased

An ordinance was passed by the General Assembly of the Commonwealth of Virginia and went into effect on this day that allowed for the lawful storage of flour in tobacco warehouses. The ordinance also provided for the inspection of flour within the borough. The rules for inspection of flour within the boundaries of the borough would be the same regulations that were used to inspect flour within the boundaries of the commonwealth.

February 7

1922—City Voters Approve Bond

On this day, Norfolk voters passed legislation to allot $5 million in funds to construct a grain elevator and a port terminal. Following World War I, it was noted that the city had no docks or wharf that would greatly aid in tapping into shipping opportunities. The facility would be built in two sections, the working house (capable of storing 224,000 million bushels) where grain would be loaded on ships and the storage house (capable of storing 523,000 million bushels) where the grain was stored before being moved to the working house. Bids were opened for the project on April 26 at noon.

February 8

1877—City's Finest Ferried to Fête

At 9:00 p.m., the steamer *N.P. Banks* of the Old Dominion Steamship Line departed Chamberlaine's Wharf for the navy yard in Portsmouth for the "most fashionable gathering that Norfolk had for a long time boasted of." A naval ball was given for the grand dukes and naval officers of Russian vessels *Swetlana* and *Bogatyr.* During the program, dancers performed quadrilles, several waltzes, polkas, a galop (faster than a polka and usually in $^2/_4$ time) and ended with the Virginia Reel. As a memento of the affair, attendees could take home a handsome dance card, printed on thick stock with gilt edges and adorned with ensigns of Russia and the United States. The card was held together by silk cords with tassels at the end. The newspapers aptly described the dresses and accessories of the lovely ladies who attended.

February 9

2006—Norfolk Men Meet with Marlins President

Two men from Norfolk, businessman Will Somerindyke Jr. and attorney Jack Kane, hosted an official from the Florida Marlins baseball team to let him know that the city would be interested in having the team relocate to the Mermaid City. Norfolk and Hampton Roads as a whole still lacked a major league sports team despite a large metropolitan and sports-friendly population. San Antonio, Texas, and Portland, Oregon, were other towns that courted the Marlins.

February 10

1963—Songstress Misses Concert

Dinah Washington and her three-piece male backup band the Allegros were scheduled to perform an afternoon concert as a scholarship fundraiser for Delta Sigma Theta sorority at Norfolk State College. The event, which had been heavily advertised, was to take place at the Norfolk Arena, but a glitch at LaGuardia Airport in New York delayed Washington's arrival. Although an offer was made to reschedule for the following day, the Deltas refused, explaining that many in the audience of 3,500 had traveled great distances to attend. The sorority young ladies refunded money to ticket holders, although some graciously refused, claiming scholarships were much more important.

February 11

1935—Rockabilly Notable Born

Venerable rockabilly great Gene Vincent was born in Norfolk as Vincent Eugene Craddock. He grew up in the city and, as a fan of country music, learned to play the guitar when he was twelve. At seventeen, Vincent joined the navy, but a leg injury prevented him from reenlisting. He decided to nurture his talent for music and landed a spot on *Country Showtime*, a local live Friday night broadcast on country radio station WCMS. He signed with Capital Records in 1956, and his single "Be-Bop-a-Lula" stayed on the charts for twenty weeks, making it to number seven. Vincent died in California from a ruptured ulcer in 1971. In 1997, Vincent was the first inductee into the Rockabilly Hall of Fame. He also holds a place in the Rock and Roll Hall of Fame.

February 12

1960—Student Sit-Ins Spread to Norfolk

Less than two weeks after four students from Agricultural and Technical College of North Carolina (now known as North Carolina A&T University) took their seats at a segregated lunch counter in Greensboro, North Carolina, a group of thirty-eight students from Norfolk State College (now known as Norfolk State University) staged a demonstration at the Woolworths on Granby Street. The young people occupied the seats at the lunch counter from 5:30 to 6:10 p.m. and then left peacefully. This was one of a number of peaceful sit-ins staged by students from black colleges, universities and even high schools. Within two months, the movement reached fifty-four cities in nine states.

February 13

1905—Postal Inspectors to Examine Altered Pouches

Two sealed packages containing mail pouches that had been found with their straps cut awaited the thoughtful eye of Special Agent Bulla. One was discovered abandoned not far from the Norfolk Post Office, and the other turned up on a Portsmouth pier. A mail pouch had been reported missing in Newport News a month earlier, but it was not known if that pouch was one of those held at Norfolk. It was suspected that items of value had been removed from the tampered bags.

February 14

1900—Annual Library Meeting Held

At the annual meeting of the president and board of directors of the Norfolk Library, it was reported that there was an increase in visitation, circulation and membership. In 1899, 662 volumes were added to the collection, two-thirds of which were purchased and the remainder donated. Because of increased use in the reading rooms and limited storage space, librarian W.H. Sargeant recommended a new building, which he believed would be achieved by "an appeal to the public spirit of our citizens." It was agreed that a committee be formed for the purpose of collecting subscriptions for the purchase of a lot on which to build a new library.

February 15

2006—School Board Budget Expands Pre-K Classes

The Norfolk School Board's proposed $311.3 million budget included adding five more pre-kindergarten classes in city schools. Ideally, pre-K would be available at all elementary schools within city limits. The early education program was targeted to at-risk four-year-olds. State and locally appropriated dollars currently supported the program, which served over 1,600 city youngsters. The additional five classes would reach ninety children. School superintendent Stephen C. Jones said that early education programs were an "investment that pays big, big dividends."

February 16

1989—Norfolk Mace Transported to Chrysler Museum

Norfolk's sterling silver mace, bestowed to the city in 1754 by Lieutenant Governor Robert Dinwiddie, was transported to the Chrysler Museum to be placed on permanent display. The mace was protected during both the American Revolution, when it was removed from the city, and the Civil War, when it was hidden under a fireplace in a home that was later used by Union soldiers. It was brought out for special ceremonies, such as the Jamestown Exposition in 1907 and the 250th anniversary of the founding of the city in 1932.

February 17

1866—Resumption of Norfolk and Petersburg Railroad Celebrated

Great rejoicing took place as riders from Richmond and Petersburg arrived via rail to mark the return of the operation of the Norfolk and Petersburg Railroad. When the guests pulled into the station at the corner of New Castle and East Main Streets at 10:00 p.m., they were greeted by a celebratory crowd led by Mayor Tabb. On board the arriving train were Governor Pierpont and a throng of senators and members of the House of Delegates. The event marked what was hoped to be an "omen of brighter promise." Introductions were made, and the distinguished crowd dined at W.S. Pepper's on Main Street. After-dinner speeches and toasts were enhanced and bolstered by Pepper's wine. In the end, it was reported that "the mountaineers, relished oysters; the piedmont men, mountain dew; and the seaboard men, everything that came their way."

February 18

2011—City Withdraws Support for Midtown Office Tower

Days after backing a project to build a $32.7 million, 165,000-square-foot office tower at the corner of Tidewater Drive and Virginia Beach Boulevard, City Manager Marcus Jones announced that the plans were off. The project fizzled after officials learned that Southeastern Tidewater Opportunity Project (STOP), the nonprofit organization that was believed to be the primary occupier of the new office space, could not afford the new digs. STOP instead planned to move to smaller quarters at Norfolk Commerce Park.

February 19

1979—German Defense Minister Arrives in Norfolk

Despite foul weather, West German defense minister Hans Apel and entourage flew into Norfolk International Airport aboard a Luftwaffe 707, the first stop on their four-day trip to the United States. He was met by the commander of the U.S. fleet, Admiral Harry D. Train III, who accompanied Apel on a helicopter trip to the naval base and a tour of the submarine USS *Casimir Pulaski*. It was Minister Apel's first visit to the United States and came after an invitation from U.S. Secretary of Defense Harold Brown.

February 20

1818—Firing of Guns Prohibited Within Boundaries of Borough

On this day, the Common Council of the Borough of Norfolk passed an ordinance that prohibited the firing of guns within the limits of the borough. Among the firearms prohibited from discharging under the new ordinance were guns, pistols and fowling pieces. A five-dollar penalty would be charged to anyone who broke the law. The new regulation went into effect immediately after its passage.

February 21

1922—Dirigible Roma *Founders and Crashes*

Thirty-four men died when the 410-foot dirigible airship *Roma* crashed while flying over Norfolk. The Italian-built *Roma* was purchased by the U.S. government for the Army Air Service and was shipped to America. When it arrived and was unpacked, officials from Langley Air Force Base on the Virginia Peninsula noted that the airship was weakened by mildew. It made its first American flight on November 15, 1921. On this day in history, the *Roma* was

Twisted wreckage of the airship *Roma*. *Courtesy Sargeant Memorial Collection, Norfolk Public Library.*

flying from Langley Field when it began to nosedive. Witnesses reported crew members throwing heavy objects from the airship to prevent a rapid descent. *Roma* ran into electrical lines and burst into flames.

February 22

1878—President's Birthday Once Again Observed

After a hiatus during and after the Civil War, George Washington's birthday was once again celebrated in the city. The day coincided with the fiftieth anniversary of Norfolk Light Artillery Blues, a prestigious state militia unit that fought in several important battles during the war. The festivities for the day included a military parade through both Norfolk and Portsmouth and a fifty-gun salute. The "Blues" and the Norfolk City Guard were joined by the Lynchburg Home Guard, whose members traveled to the city by train.

February 23

2010—Bookie Reaches Plea Deal, Steers Clear of Clinker

A well-known Norfolk bookmaker involved in gambling since the 1960s pleaded guilty to one count of running an illegal gambling operation and testified to running an illegal betting business for five years. The eighty-two-year-old agreed to a plea deal in Federal Court in which he would give up over $1 million in cash and goods. The deal allowed the longtime bookmaker to avoid serving any time in prison.

February 24

1936—Colley Theater Opens on Street Named Same

On this day, the five-hundred-seat Art Deco Colley Theater, considered a "suburban theater" at that time, opened for business. Its first feature film was *A Midsummer Night's Dream* starring James Cagney and Olivia DeHaviland in the film based on the Shakespeare play. Portsmouth-born William S. Wilder opened the Colley after working in many downtown movie theaters during the dawn of the golden age of cinema. The lessons he learned early on would help his business ventures. Prior to opening the Colley (which was renamed the Naro in the 1960s), Wilder opened the Newport Theater on Thirty-fifth Street in 1928.

February 25

1937—Scores of Tickets Issued as City Starts Parking Meter Trial

Estimates of between 250 and 400 parking tickets were issued on the first day of a ninety-day trial period for parking meters in the downtown area. Over two hundred meters were installed on Granby Street from Bute Street to City Hall Avenue and on cross streets from Boush Street to Monticello Avenue. A nickel bought an hour of parking. The fine for overparking was a dollar per hour, which could be paid at police headquarters. A group of local businessmen vehemently fought the installation of the meters.

February 26

1920—Norfolk Shipping Interests Hold New York Conference

A delegation of Norfolk businessmen headed to New York City to meet with H.B. Walker, president of the Old Dominion Line. The rushed get-together took place after the steamship line was obtained by the Clyde-Mallory Line, and it was feared that the Old Dominion steamers would no longer provide service on the James River between Richmond and Norfolk. Farmers depended on river traffic to carry goods farther south than the capital city. The Richmond Chamber of Commerce did not mirror Norfolk in sending men to lobby for the continuance of the traffic between the two cities, but it sent a telegram to Mr. Walker questioning his plans. Even Governor Westmorland Davis, speaking as a citizen and not in an official capacity, said that he would "deplore anything that would tend to cripple or inconvenience the commerce of Virginia."

February 27

1986—AIDS Victims Cancel Interview

After a WNIS radio host expressed an irrational fear of the Acquired Immune Deficiency Syndrome (AIDS), two people exposed to the virus chose not to grant an interview. A representative of the Tidewater AIDS Crisis Task Force said, "We certainly do not wish to force our cause upon a group that apparently has not educated themselves on the transmission of the AIDS virus." The WNIS interview did eventually take place, albeit over the phone. Henry Del Toro, of WNOR, expressed dismay over WNIS's decision. "I think it makes them look really bad. He comes off as a buffoon," the outspoken disc jockey Del Toro said of the fearful and misinformed WNIS broadcaster. Del Toro also interviewed the subject, who went by the air name of "John." In on the interview was regional health director, Dr. William B. Crawford, who reiterated that AIDS was not spread through casual contact.

February 28

1899—Red Stockings Meet and Organize for Season

The city's famed independent black baseball team, the Red Stockings, held an organizational meeting for the upcoming season. The squad already had games scheduled, including one in Chicago. The Red Stockings would begin practice in April, and mangers let it be known that the team would "consider all challenges." On the roster were W. Parker, first base and captain; John McClennan, Charles James and James Lewis, catchers; Daniel McClennan, Caleb Minton and Daniel Terry, pitchers; Charles Olds, Willie James and Wash Stewart, infielders; and Thomas Wright, William Johnson and John Burton, outfielders.

MARCH

March 1

1941—Darden Steps Down

On this day, Colgate W. Darden Jr. vacated his congressional seat, to which he had been elected four (although nonconsecutive) times, in order to run for governor of Virginia. The forty-four-year-old Darden, a Norfolk lawyer, World War I veteran and Democrat, had announced his candidacy earlier. On Election Day, Darden defeated his Republican, Communist and Socialist opponents overwhelmingly, collecting over 80 percent of the vote. He served as governor of the Old Dominion from January 1942 to January 1946. Darden was also known for his contributions to education. He served as the third chancellor of the University of Virginia from 1947 to 1959, and prior to that, he was involved with the College of William and Mary.

March 2

1980—Snow Traps Circus-Goers at Scope

Norfolk was in the throes of a snowy winter and had already experienced four snowfalls totaling over twenty-eight inches. Ringling Brothers Circus was in town for a five-day run at Scope arena and was scheduled to end its stay with three performances each on Saturday and Sunday. On Saturday, snow began to fall and continued into the evening. The following day, more than one thousand people attended the morning show that ended midafternoon. By evening, the new snow total for the season was nearly forty inches. Afternoon circus goers, over two thousand people, were told it would be too dangerous to leave Scope. While some tried to make it home in their vehicles or walked home, many spent the night downtown. In order to entertain the captive crowd, a final performance of the circus was given on that evening.

March 3

1972—Former Mayor Killed by Gunfire

W. Fred Duckworth, a member of the Virginia State Highway Commission and former Norfolk mayor, was shot six times approximately a half-mile from the Algonquin House, a high-rise apartment building where he lived with his wife. Forty detectives were called to aid in the investigation following the shooting. The seventy-two-year-old Duckworth was not carrying a wallet, and two expensive rings were not removed from his body, ruling robbery out as a reason for the killing. It was not unusual for him to take neighborhood walks at night.

March 4

1897—Runaway Horse Subdued

East Main Street had a flurry of activity when a horse that was leading a wagon of the Adam's Express became a runaway. The incident took place around 9:00 a.m. The horse and wagon in question collided with another wagon, causing two young men to be thrown into the street. The pileup was enough to stop the out-of-control animal, which was then captured. The boys were not seriously injured, and minimal damage was sustained by the two vehicles involved.

March 5

1934—CCC Librarian Dies Following Errant Stabbing

Stewart DeGroat of Middletown, New York, died in a Norfolk hospital of wounds received when he was stabbed on a Norfolk street two days earlier. The black youth was stationed with Civilian Conservation Corps (CCC)

Company 1371 at Cape Henry and was on leave from camp with other CCC boys when a drunk accosted the group. After learning about their son's hospitalization, DeGroat's parents drove to Norfolk to be by his side, but the nineteen-year-old died before they arrived. The young man's body was sent home aboard a train.

March 6

2001—City Council Regulates Alcohol Sales

After a public outcry from neighborhood leaders, Norfolk City Council voted to amend an ordinance that would require a permit for new businesses that planned to sell alcohol. The amendment also allowed for more neighborhood input that might help determine where off-site sales establishments would be located and how close to one another they could operate. Businesses that sold off-site liquor would now be governed by the same law that governed adult businesses such as adult bookstores, movie theaters and massage parlors.

March 7

1962—Ash Wednesday Storm Pounds Coast and Low-Lying Areas

An unusual mix of astronomic influences came together to create a storm of extraordinary proportion. A lingering low pressure system combined with spring tides that were running higher than normal. Low-lying areas of Norfolk and Portsmouth were inundated with floodwater. The bay-front neighborhoods of Ocean View and Willoughby faced the storm head on. It was said that one thousand people evacuated those communities, including a family of seven down with the measles. The Ash Wednesday Storm, dubbed so by Outer Banks publicist Aycock Brown, was a maelstrom endured from the North Carolina coast to the Jersey Shore. Virginia's Chincoteague Island was especially hard hit.

March 8

*1862—*Merrimack *Destorys Union Gun Boats*

The Confederate ironclad *Virginia*, formerly the USS *Merrimack*, left the Gosport Navy Yard across the river from Norfolk and headed to Hampton Roads to call on the ships of the federal blockade squadron. After delivering a broadside shot to the USS *Congress*, it fired on the USS *Cumberland*, the heaviest armed ship in the U.S. Navy, and sank it after ramming it squarely. The *Merrimack* then dueled with the *Congress* for almost an hour until the *Congress* struck its colors and headed toward shore, but it was captured and later burned. It was written that the ship ablaze "was witnessed by thousands of spectators from our harbors and shores." Close to midnight, the fire reached the *Congress*'s magazine and shattered the night with a great *ka-boom*. The following day, the *Virginia* would spar with the USS *Monitor* in the first-ever Battle of the Ironclads.

The destruction of the USS *Cumberland* by the Confederate ironclad *Virginia*, formerly the *Merrimack. Library of Congress.*

March 9

1932—Preeminent Jazz Singer Born

Dorothy Jaqueline Keely was born and raised in Norfolk. When she was about ten years old, she joined *Joe Brown's Radio Gang*, an on-air radio show. A new song was learned weekly, and on the weekends, the songsters traveled to local military installations to perform for servicemen. An audition was arranged with the Norfolk Naval Air Station Band, and Dorothy was offered a spot. She later became known professionally as Keely Smith. Her best-known work was with her husband of eight years (1953–61), band leader Louis Prima. Smith played the straight man to Prima's onstage kookiness. After the couple's divorce, she remarried and focused on raising her daughters. Smith played both "rooms" and "lounges," claiming that rooms were nicer, but lounges offered longer terms of employment.

March 10

1913—Laundrymen Convene in City

Mayor W.R. Mayo gave the opening welcome at the spring meeting of the Virginia and West Virginia Laundrymen's Association, which took place in Norfolk. The group was created to share information on how best to serve its customer base. A representative from Baltimore's Munsey publishing organization addressed the group about advertising. Following the morning session, conventioneers were shown around the city by members of the Tidewater Automobile Association. Local men in the laundry business hosted a banquet that night.

March 11

2003—Batten Makes Donation to Old Dominion University

Media mogul and Norfolk native Frank Batten made a substantial donation to Old Dominion University, where he served as the school's first rector. The $32 million gift was the largest donation ever made to ODU and came at the beginning of a major capital campaign. While all departments of the university would benefit from the donation, the following fall, the new

School of Engineering and Technology was named in Batten's honor. His citizenship, leadership and need to better the community were motivating factors in his life. Batten, the founder of Landmark Communications and creator of the Weather Channel, also provided for an $11.2 million gift to Virginia Wesleyan College, its largest donation as well.

March 12

1950—Pulitzer Prize–Winning Editor Dies

Louis I. Jaffé, editor of the *Virginian-Pilot* newspaper, died at a Norfolk hospital following a heart attack. Jaffé, a native of Detroit, was educated in North Carolina, and in 1929, he was awarded the Pulitzer Prize for distinguished editorial writing for a series of editorials that were instrumental in the passing of a Virginia anti-lynching law. Jaffé, the son of Jewish immigrants from Lithuania, denounced other organizations and causes, including the KKK, the religious right interfering with the teaching of evolution and the state's Racial Integrity Law. He worked with Plummer Bernard Young, editor of the city's black newspaper, *Norfolk Journal and Guide*, to work toward elevating conditions for blacks and improving race relations. At the time of his death, Louis I. Jaffé was sixty-two years old.

March 13

1921—Coast Guard to Add to Fleet

Press reports announced that the U.S. Coast Guard would assign two additional tugboats to its station in Norfolk. The steel oceangoing tugboat *Winnisimmit*, formerly ported at Boston, and the smaller tug *Relief* from Baltimore would join the tug *Chowan* in Norfolk and would bring three total tugs to the city. In addition to the tugboats, the Coast Guard cutter *Manning* also called Norfolk home.

March 14

1906—Accused Murderer Takes Own Life

A twenty-nine-year-old man, who was reportedly "formerly prominent" in Portsmouth but now rejected by his friends and family, cut his throat with a very sharp and smuggled penknife in his Norfolk jail cell. He was accused of throwing a lighted lamp at a woman, which exploded, burning her severely. It was surmised his upcoming trial weighed heavily on his mind. The suicide was discovered when the fellow in the cell below reported a gurgling noise.

March 15

1975—Crowd Welcomes Running Monarchs, NCAA Division II Champs

A lively gathering of thousands of students and fans was on hand at Norfolk International Airport to welcome home Old Dominion University's Running Monarchs after they captured the NCAA Division II Basketball Championship, defeating New Orleans 76–74 in Evansville, Indiana. Approximately two thousand people traveled to the Hooiser State to cheer ODU on in the tournament. The crowd at the airport was so large that the corridor shook from the weight of those assembled. After welcoming the Monarchs at the airport, the group moved to the amphitheater at Norfolk Botanical Gardens for a program that included cheering and speeches. Wilson Washington was voted most valuable player of the final game. Team captain was Oliver Purnell, and Sonny Allen was coach.

March 16

1964—Demonstrators Protest Electricity Rates

About three dozen housewives, some with children in tow, staged a five-hour demonstration in front of the Norfolk office of the Virginia Electric and Power Company (VEPCO). The women were protesting high electric bills, and although a rate cut would go into effect on April 1, the protesters decried it as not enough and "ridiculous." They carried signs with slogans such as "Do We Heat or Do We Eat," "VEPCO Rates Are Too High" and "A Monopoly Is Against the American Way of Life." The planned rate cut would lower the average monthly household bill by twenty cents. After VEPCO went on record stating that its rates were not too high, the women planned additional demonstrations and wrote to Attorney General Robert F. Kennedy asking for support.

March 17

1909—Naval YMCA Dedicated

The new $300,000 YMCA building was dedicated on this day. It was a gift of wealthy businessman John D. Rockefeller. Author and historian William Sloane acted as master of ceremonies and read messages from Rockefeller, President Taft and Secretary of the Navy George von Lengerke Meyer. Of special note during the day was the bequest of $1,000 given by the men of the battleship USS *Virginia* and a $450 gift presented by those aboard the USS *Kentucky*. The money was to be used to furnish the new facility. A telegram was sent to Rockefeller expressing gratitude from the city, as well as from naval officers and enlisted personnel.

John D. Rockefeller was instrumental in the financing of the downtown Norfolk YMCA. *Library of Congress.*

March 18

1920—Application for Jitney Company Filed

On this day, an application was filed with the State Corporation Commission to incorporate a jitney company in Norfolk. The name of the proposed company would be Virginia Bus Company, Inc., and it would provide jitney service, meaning passenger transportation on small busses. Officers set to run the Virginia Bus Company were W.A. Traynham, president; E.A. Ross, secretary; R.J. Brown, treasurer; and L.A. Howell as general counsel.

March 19

2006—Lady Vol Enters Record Book

Candace Parker, a red-shirt freshman on the University of Tennessee's Lady Volunteers, became the first woman to ever dunk a basketball in an NCAA tournament game. The milestone came at the 6:12 mark in the Volunteers' rout against Army. The six-foot-four Parker then added to her accomplishments by becoming the first woman to dunk twice in a collegiate contest. The records were set during the first round of the 2006 NCAA Woman's Tournament. The game took place at the Ted Constant Convocation Center on the Old Dominion University campus.

March 20

1905—Black Pastors Convene to Improve Conditions for Youth

A convention of the leaders of Norfolk's black churches met for the purpose of determining ways to improve the surroundings for the city's black youth. It was noted that after serving apprenticeships in the country, young men were often drawn to the city, where they were susceptible to falling victim to "vicious company" and "social clubs of questionable character." The theme of the meeting was "The Reduction of Accessions to the Criminal Ranks."

March 21

1921—City Firemen Send Donation to Richmond Heroes Fund

W.T. Traylor, treasurer of the Norfolk Protective Association of Firefighters and member of the Norfolk Fire Department, mailed a check in the amount of one hundred dollars to benefit the children, widows and parents of four Richmond firefighters who died in a horrific blaze in the capital city. It was one of the most unfortunate fires in the city history. Six others were hospitalized from injuries sustained during the blaze. The Norfolk firemen approved the donation at a meeting the evening before.

March 22

1982—Hotel Reopens After $3.5 Million Renovation

A seventy-six-year-old refurbished downtown hotel opened as the Hotel Madison and hoped to find its niche serving business clients and hosting small corporate meetings. The hotel was built to attract travelers to the 1907 Jamestown Exposition, which marked the 300th anniversary of the first permanent English settlement in America. The name later changed to Southland and then to the Commodore Maury. When it closed in 1976, prior to its renovation, the Commodore Maury served as a rooming house and was a popular hostelry for railroad workers. Following the facelift, the Hotel Madison became the Clarion James Madison. Around 2008, it was being remodeled, but the project stumbled due to some shady deals. In 2013, developer Buddy Gadams acquired the building and breathed new life into it yet again. It has been meticulously restored as a mixed use of apartments and retail space.

March 23

1866—Music Critic Harrangued Following Negative Review

The morning that a review—less than flattering yet deemed fair—of a performance of the opera *Norma* was printed in the newspaper, the music critic for the *Norfolk Post*, James F. Milligan, of the U.S. Army Signal

Corps, was stopped on a city street and verbally harangued by members of the opera company. The accosters with "outstretched arms sawed the entranchant air most dramatically." Milligan had written, "The fiddlers were worse than the singing and the singers were worse than the stringed instruments." Additionally, there had been sentiment—especially among the city's clergy—that it was inappropriate to stage an opera during Lent.

March 24

1974—Pastor Preaches from Roof of Church

After ambling up a twenty-foot ladder with a microphone around his neck, twenty-three-year-old pastor Stephen Thornton delivered his Sunday sermon from the roof of his church after he made a deal with his congregation. He challenged members of Ocean View Church of Christ to up attendance in Sunday school and promised that he would preach from the rooftop if 125 people showed up. The theme of Thornton's homily was "A View from the Rooftop." Congregants listened from lawn chairs, the hoods of cars and while seated on the grass. The fickle Norfolk spring weather was particularly cooperative on this day.

March 25

1965—Norfolk Attorneys Recommend Liquor by the Drink

A group of four Norfolk lawyers, two of whom were also members of the Virginia House of Delegates, appeared before a special legislative commission and touted the virtues of amending liquor laws to allow liquor by the drink. All men agreed that the change would be a boon to the state's and the region's tourism industry. Charles Cooper, who spoke on behalf of the Norfolk Junior Chamber of Commerce, said the adoption of a new law was imperative "if the tourist industry in Tidewater is ever to get off its feet."

March 26

1990—Roland Park Residents Rally

Over one hundred people from the Roland Park neighborhood met with police at the Second Patrol Division in order to express concerns over recent break-ins and gang violence and to ask for increased police protection. In an effort to make the neighborhood safer, they organized a block watch program along with a civic league. Their actions had a positive effect on the neighborhood. Created in the 1950s, Roland Park is made up of just under five hundred tidy brick homes. Residents enjoy the area's sidewalks, playground and open areas.

March 27

1919—Tug Crew Jailed

The crew members of the tugboat *Henrico* of the Southern Transportation Company found themselves in jail after the vessel was determined to be carrying beer and liquor. Prohibition officers found forty-two bottles of beer and 275 pint bottles of whiskey in the *Henrico*'s hold. The vessel was seized until the case went to court.

March 28

*1907—*Connecticut *Sailors Commandeer Passenger Vessel*

While returning from Norfolk to Old Point Comfort aboard the steamer *Ocean View*, one hundred sailors (more or less) described as boisterous in nature from the battleship *Connecticut* overtook the vessel, overpowering the captain, crew, firemen, deckhands and engineers. The mariners had been on leave in Norfolk and were reportedly "doing the town" while there. Windows were broken, and rookie seamen drove the cooks from the galley in order to grab whatever snacks they could. The frightened passengers were thankful when the *Ocean View* neared shore, and the vigilantes gave control of the ship back to the proper authorities.

March 29

1893—Message From Ill-Fated Naronic *Found*

A watchman at Ocean View discovered a message in a bottle, which relayed the plight of the steamship *Naronic.* According to the note, the ship had hit an iceberg and some of the crew and passengers made it into lifeboats, but time was running out. The message also urged that the agents of the ship *M. Kersey* of New York be notified. This was the second message found mentioning the *Naronic.* Neither of the notes had signatures that matched actual passengers from the ship's manifest. The *Naronic* was sailing from Liverpool, England, to New York. Its fate remains unknown.

March 30

2010—Council Votes to Aquire Panda for Krocs

Norfolk City Council approved a $900,000 expenditure to purchase the Panda Chinese Restaurant on Princess Anne Road, property needed for the planned Kroc Center, a recreation facility of the Salvation Army built in part by funds from a bequest of Joan Kroc, wife of McDonald's founder Ray Kroc. Salvation Army leaders worked with local officials to ensure the project would come to be. Local fundraising efforts, led by Joshua P. Darden and Frank Batten Jr., procured $25 million that were matched with an $80 million Kroc bequest. Ground was broken in 2012, and the 92,000-square-foot complex at the corner of Ballentine Boulevard and Princess Anne Road was completed two years later.

March 31

1895—Consolidation Considered, New Names Suggested

As a follow-up to an editorial in the *Norfolk Virginian*, which suggested a new moniker for the "Greater Norfolk" area, letters were published with suggestions for new names. At the time, Berkley, an incorporated town on the south side of the Elizabeth River, was being eyed for annexation. The extension was finalized in 1906. "Triopolis" was suggested as a name to represent the combined area of Norfolk, Portsmouth and Berkley. Another name put forth in a letter to the editor was Doublein, perhaps hinting that the city wanted to double in size. Norberport or Norber Port were suggestions from Roanoke, Virginia, that combined all three place names.

APRIL

April 1

1754—Silver Mace Is Gift of Lieutenant Governor

Robert Dinwiddie, Virginia's royal lieutenant governor, presented a silver ceremonial mace to the Borough of Norfolk, the largest town in the Commonwealth. The sterling silver mace was crafted by the English silversmith Fuller White and made of eleven interlocking pieces. The finished work was described as "very handsome" and "thankfully received" in the minutes of the Norfolk Common Council. It measured over forty-one inches and weighed six and a half pounds. The mace, believed to be the oldest municipal mace still in the city for which it was created, has a rich history tied to important events in city, state and national history.

April 2

1950—WTAR Brings Televison to Hampton Roads

Virginia's second television station, WTAR, took to the airwaves. Announcers read news stories taken from the national news wire reports. Originally assigned to channel 4 and primarily an NBC affiliate, WTAR broadcast programs from the four networks of the time, ABC, NBC, CBS and DuMont. Two years later, the station moved to channel 3 and, in 1957, became affiliated with CBS. The station changed to WTKR in the early 1980s after being sold to Knight-Ridder.

April 3

1947—Whale of a Controversy Brews in Little Creek

A wayward whale caught the enterprising eye of the Norfolk Tallow Company when it became stranded in Little Creek. Norfolk Tallow wanted to tow the whale and render its valuable oil but needed the beast subdued. After the eighty-foot sea mammal nicknamed Blackie went dormant for a spell, it was assumed it was dead, but after a good rest the following day, he began to flip and flap and slap and spout. At first request, both the navy and the Coast Guard declined to aid in Blackie's demise, but after it appeared the sea denizen would never make it back to deep water, military bullets aided in bringing Blackie's life to a close.

April 4

1930—Academy of Music Burns

Firefighters battle a blaze that destroyed the Academy of Music on Main Street. *Photo by Charles Borjes, courtesy Sargeant Memorial Collection, Norfolk Public Library.*

Norfolk's Academy of Music, located downtown on Main Street, suffered from an immense fire of unknown origin that left only the brick exterior standing. It was reported that the theater was one of the oldest in the city and had been in operation for fifty years. A valiant effort was shown to keep the downtown blaze from spreading to other businesses, including thousands of feet of fire hose engaged and the use of the city fire boat *Vulcan*. The fire, estimated to cause $100,000 in damage, originated in the theater's dome, most likely due to bad wiring.

April 5

1905—Kidnapped Boy Erroneously Reported as Found

Newspapers reported that an eight-year-old boy, Kenneth Beasley, who mysteriously disappeared while on his way home from school six weeks prior, was found in Norfolk. The kidnapping victim was the son of state senator S.M. Beasley from Currituck County, North Carolina, just south of the Virginia–North Carolina border. The news reports were false. Joshua Harrison, whose views on liquor regulation differed with Beasley's, was later found guilty of the kidnapping and, while waiting for an appeal from the state supreme court, killed himself at Norfolk's Gladstone Hotel. Harrison left a letter declaring his innocence.

April 6

1889—Strong Winds Damage Roofs, Bring Flooding

What began as an early-season hail-bearing thunderstorm ended in an all-night windstorm that blew a record eighteen-inch flood tide into Norfolk Harbor and accompanying waterways. It was the highest tide ever recorded and was driven by northwest winds over fifty miles per hour. The wind's force could be seen on the roofs of several city buildings. A fire broke out on Water Street and burned over one thousand bales of cotton and additional goods along with damaging other businesses. Portsmouth also suffered from a fire that burned a lumberyard.

April 7

2007—Multimillion-Dollar Cruise Center Opens

City officials and citizens were on hand for the opening of the Halfe Moon Cruise and Celebration Center, the eighty-thousand-square-foot passenger terminal and welcome center for the city's cruise industry. Concerts and demonstrations were part of the festivities marking the day. The first vessel to use the state-of-the-art facility located adjacent to Nauticus was Royal Caribbean's *Empress of the Seas*, which arrived at the end of the month. The center also offered indoor and outdoor event space for weddings, conferences and meetings with incomparable views of the Elizabeth River. During its first six years, the facility generated over $8 million in direct revenue with additional indirect revenues in hotel and restaurant traffic.

April 8

1983—Tenor Returns to Sing for Classical Concert

Charles Holland, a seventy-three-year-old classically trained vocalist, returned to his hometown to sing with the Virginia Philharmonic. Holland was coached during the 1920s by May Henley, who urged the talented black vocalist to leave Norfolk in order to pursue his career as an opera singer because it would never be realized in a segregated city. The concert was arranged after Holland, who was in New York to sing at Carnegie Hall, mentioned to a reporter from *Newsweek* magazine that he would like to sing in his hometown. Holland was honored by city officials. He said Mrs. Henley's spirit had remained with him throughout his noted career.

April 9

1911—Philanthropist Dines with Sailors

Miss Helen Gould had Sunday dinner with hundreds of enlisted men and shook hands with over two thousand sailors on leave from the USS *Louisiana* and USS *New Hampshire*. The dinner was held at the Naval YMCA. Gould, who had been referred to as a "bluejacket's best friend," had a history of pledging monetary support to the military causes and was also a supporter of the YMCA and YWCA. When asked by an officer to share a meal in a private dining room, the forty-two-year-old heiress expressed her preference for dining "with the boys."

April 10

1936—Alcohol Permit Suspensions Go Into Effect

Following a hearing in Richmond, the Virginia Alcohol Beverage Control (ABC) Board addressed problems of rowdiness and disorderliness in drinking establishments, dubbed "beer gardens," in the city's East Main Street district. One establishment had its license revoked, while nine others had their permits indefinitely suspended. An ABC official reported the scene as such: "You have seen wild places in the movies and read of wild places in books, but until you see Norfolk, you haven't seen anything."

April 11

1964—Decorated General Is Honored

After lying in state in Washington and New York, the body of General Douglas MacArthur proceeded past hundreds of citizens who lined the streets of Norfolk. MacArthur felt a connection to the city since his mother, Mary Pinckney Hardy MacArthur, grew up at Riversedge, the family plantation near the Berkley section, and his brother and several uncles were buried in Cedar Grove Cemetery. He had arranged to be buried in the restored old Norfolk City Hall building. Over sixty thousand citizens paid respect to the body while it lay under the old city hall dome. On April 11, MacArthur's casket was driven down City Hall Avenue to St. Paul's Church for a simple service attended by four hundred mourners. Representing President Lyndon Baines Johnson was U.S. attorney general Robert F. Kennedy and his wife, Ethel.

April 12

1974—WFL Team Claims Norfolk and Foreman Field

The Washington Ambassadors of the World Football League (WFL) announced that they would change their name to the Virginia Ambassadors and play their home games at Foreman Field. The franchise originally planned to use Robert F. Kennedy Stadium in Washington, D.C., but was blocked by the National Football League's Washington Redskins, who already called RFK home. Before deciding on Norfolk, Ambassadors owners attempted negotiations to play in Annapolis at Navy–Marine Corps Stadium but needed lights for the field. Officials promised to bring in at least two big-name players to the team. The Ambassadors' schedule included twenty games, ten of which would be played in Norfolk.

April 13

1922—Massive Fire Destroys Berkley

A great blaze, described in some newspaper accounts as a holocaust, burned more than one hundred homes and left five hundred families without shelter. The fire destroyed a section in the Norfolk suburb of Berkley a mile long and between two and four blocks wide. Tunis Lumber Mills on the Elizabeth River was ground zero for the fire, and at least two steamers nearby perished in the blaze. Homes, churches and businesses were wiped out. The damage was estimated at over $1 million.

Some of those left homeless by the Great Berkley Fire. *Photo by Charles Borjes, courtesy Sargeant Memorial Collection, Norfolk Public Library.*

April 14

1993—Tides Open at New Stadium with New Name

The former Tidewater Tides, now called the Norfolk Tides, played their home opener in the new $16 million, twelve-thousand-seat baseball stadium, Harbor Park. The change in name for the International League team came about because the city paid for much of the construction of the downtown waterfront venue. Although a punch-list of finishing touches still needed to be completed and the stadium restaurant would take another month to complete, the field and seats were ready for the fans. A sell-out crowd watched the Tides blank the Ottawa Lynx 2–0.

April 15

1899—New Freighter Makes Inaugural Trip

The four-deck freight steamer *Kershaw* of the Merchants and Miners Line made its first trip and arrived from Baltimore. The 274-foot ship built chiefly of iron at Wilmington, Delaware, was described as "an excellent vessel in every particular" and was scheduled to make runs between Baltimore, Norfolk and Boston. Several of the top officials of the Merchant and Miners Line were aboard the vessel when it made its way to port. By the afternoon, the *Kershaw* was already back at sea, heading to Providence, Rhode Island. It would enjoy a career that spanned almost three decades before colliding with the liner *President Garfield* off Martha's Vineyard with a loss of seven lives.

The battleship USS *Wisconsin* on the day it was transferred from the navy to the City of Norfolk to become a focal point and visitor attraction at Nauticus. *Photo by Seaman Scott Pittman, April 16, 2010, courtesy of DVIDS.*

April 16

2001—USS Wisconsin *Opens for Deck Tours*

The battleship USS *Wisconsin* opened for tours on this day, the anniversary of its commissioning in 1944. The 887-foot vessel was built at the Philadelphia Naval Shipyard and was christened in December 1943, two years after the bombing of Pearl Harbor. It saw duty in World

War II and in the Korean War. Its last duty was in Operation Desert Storm in 1990. The Iowa-class battleship was brought to Norfolk as an anchor piece to its downtown attraction, Nauticus. It arrived on December 7, 2000, the anniversary of its launching. Over two and a half million people have visited this floating museum since it berthed at Norfolk. On April 16, 2010, it was formally transferred to the City of Norfolk.

April 17

2001—Prince Rocks the Norva

The Norva Theater on Monticello Avenue was wrapping up its first year after a $6 million renovation. On this day, it welcomed Prince on his thirty-three-performance Hit and Run Tour. A sold-out crowd watched the legendary guitarist open with Purple Rain and play several other favorites such as Controversy, Little Red Corvette and Baby I'm a Star. Tickets cost $65.00 and were rumored to have sold out in five minutes. The Norva began as a vaudeville venue in 1917 and also enjoyed a long run as a movie theater and an athletic club before receiving a major overhaul and reopening to become one of America's premiere concert spots.

April 18

1972—Virginia Symphony Christens Chrysler Hall

The fifty-second season of the Virginia Symphony opened as the first performance in the new Chrysler Hall, a 2,500-seat performing arts center adjacent to Norfolk Scope. Tickets for the premier seats fetched twenty-five dollars. The *Virginian-Pilot* later called the evening "a momentous night in the history of culture in southeast Virginia." Currently, Chrysler Hall is home venue to the Virginia Symphony, the Virginia Ballet, the Norfolk Forum, Broadway Across America and the Virginia Arts Festival. It also hosts a variety of other concerts and shows.

April 19

1989—USS Iowa *Families Congregate On Base*

Following a morning explosion aboard the battleship *Iowa* that claimed the life of forty-seven sailors, family members of some of the ship's 1,600 crew members gathered at the Norfolk Naval Base to await news about their loved ones. The forty-six-year-old *Iowa* was on maneuvers in the open sea some three hundred miles off Puerto Rico when the explosion occurred during routine gunnery practice. According to official naval policy, before the names of the dead and injured were released, family members first needed to be notified.

April 20

1890—Pan-American Delegates Meet Norfolk Delegates

Officials attending the first-ever Pan-American Congress held in Washington, D.C., arrived at Old Point Comfort by train and then transferred to steamer USS *Despatch* and headed to Norfolk. Midway, the *Despatch* was met by a tugboat carrying an official government delegation from the city, including Mayor Colonel William Lamb and *Norfolk Landmark* editor Kenton C. Murray. Because of a strong blow, many ships were anchored at Hampton Roads, giving the Pan-American visitors ample opportunity to view the area's rich maritime industry. The guests were transferred to carriages and driven around the principal streets of the city, which was decorated for the occasion. The group then traveled by train to Virginia Beach. A delay in the trip from Washington caused the Norfolk portion of the visit originally scheduled for Saturday to be scaled back and added to the Sunday itinerary. In keeping with the tone of that day, there was little fanfare.

April 21

2007—Legendary Coach Honored

A memorial service was held at Granby High School to honor wrestling coach Billy Martin, a legend in the sport. During his tenure at Granby from 1949 to 1970, the school chalked up twenty-one state titles. In the 1960s,

Granby lost just two matches. Martin is credited with creating the wrestling move called the Granby Roll. His coaching and mentoring prepared several individuals to compete in collegiate and Olympic matches. Following the service, a reception was held at Ocean View Fishing Pier Restaurant. Martin is buried at Woodlawn Cemetery.

April 22

1932—Norfolkian Goes to Sea, Claims to Aid in Return of Lindbergh Baby

Shipbuilder John Hughes Curtis, Episcopal rector H. Dobson-Peacock and retired admiral Guy H. Burrage made up a group dubbed the Norfolk Trio or the Norfolk Negotiators, and they were involved in a cruel hoax. For over a month, Curtis had been in communication with Charles A. Lindbergh, claiming that he had been contacted by the kidnappers of Lindbergh's two-year-old son. On this day, Curtis left Norfolk aboard the yacht *Marcon*, loaned to him by his friend Colonel Charles H. Consolvo. Curtis lied to Colonel Lindbergh, alleging that the kidnappers wanted to exchange the baby for ransom money at sea. The trio's story would raise suspicion when the child's body was discovered on May 12. Curtis would make a written confession of his wrongdoing on May 16.

April 23

1966—Prominent Physician Passes

Dr. Walter Bramblette Martin, a noted physician and past president of the American Medical Association, died at his Norfolk home. Martin was a native of Pulaski in the western part of Virginia. His career, both in medicine and as a civic leader, spanned from 1919, when he began his practice, to his retirement in 1964. During World War II, Martin served in the Pacific Theater, went ashore after the invasion at Okinawa and served as a medical consultant there. At the time of his death, Dr. Martin was seventy-eight.

April 24

1844—The Great Compromiser Henry Clay Visits City

The Honorable Henry Clay, the great statesman from Kentucky, visited the city and attended a reception held in his honor. Several military organizations "paraded in grand procession," and the Norfolk Light Artillery Blues "fired a salute of twenty-six guns." Clay, known as the Great Compromiser for his ability to find common ground between members of Congress from different sections of the expanding nation, was the guest of Colonel Myer Meyers, who lived on the corner of Bank and Freemason Streets.

April 25

2002—USS Cole *Returns to Norfolk*

The USS *Cole* returned to Naval Station Norfolk following a fourteen-month stay at Northrup Grumman's Ingalls Shipyard at Pascagoula, Mississippi, where the ship received $250 million in repairs. The USS *Cole* was bombed in Yemen on October 12, 2000. The ship suffered the loss of seventeen crew members. The tragedy was deeply felt in Norfolk and by the American people. A crowd made up of relatives of those lost in the tragedy, former crew members, and others were on hand to welcome the *Cole* home.

April 26

1907—Jamestown Exposition Opens, Roosevelt Addresses Crowd

President Theodore Roosevelt addressed the large crowd on the opening day of the Jamestown Exposition at Sewell's Point, the eight-month event held commemorating the 300th anniversary of the landing of the English at Jamestown. Roosevelt is credited with averting disaster after the crowd surged toward the grandstand after the president's introduction. Roosevelt appealed to the men of Virginia "to live up to their tradition of gallantry" and to stop endangering the lives of women and children. This worked for a short time, but the crowd wanted to

President Theodore Roosevelt addresses the crowd at the opening of the Jamestown Exposition. *Library of Congress.*

hear the president's speech and again pressed forward. Members of the U.S. Cavalry were brought in and successfully "relieved the pressure" of the crowd.

April 27

1971—Cruise Line Plans Voyages to Caribbean

A press conference was held to announce that the Cunard *Adventurer*, a seven-hundred-passenger ship under construction in Rotterdam, Germany, would arrive in Norfolk the following year for twenty-six weekly cruises to San Juan, Puerto Rico, and St. Thomas, Virgin Islands. The *Adventurer* would set off from Norfolk International Terminals on Saturday evenings and return the following Saturday morning between the end of May and early November. Ticket prices for the seven-day voyage started at $240. "The Cunard *Adventurer* and the port of Norfolk are meant for each other," announced Richard B. Patton of the Cunard Line.

April 28

1973—Azalea Festival Celebrates Twenty Years

Floats and bands participated in the annual Azalea Festival Parade, which was celebrating its twentieth anniversary. There were 115 entrants from a variety of states, including Pennsylvania, West Virginia, Maryland and New Jersey, who walked and marched the parade route in an event that lasted three hours. Former area prisoners of war served as parade grand marshals. The Azalea Queen for the twentieth anniversary festival was Canada's Heather McDonald. The festival was created in conjunction with the formation of NATO's Supreme Allied Command Atlantic (SACLANT). Azalea Queens were chosen from the countries representing SACLANT.

April 29

1899—Funds Raised for Synagogue

Members of the congregation of the Chief Sholem Synagogue enjoyed the final night of a bazaar held to dispose of items left over from a recent fundraising fair. The money procured this night would be used to build a new synagogue. Several items were raffled off, including a refrigerator, a china closet, a grand piano, a sewing machine and an oil painting entitled *Vestal Virgin*. The congregation desired to build a new house of worship away from streetcar lines, which were noisy and interfered with services. Although a lot had already been purchased, it was speculated it would be sold because of expansion of city streets and that "another lot will have to be bought in a more secluded and quiet section of the city" for the new synagogue.

April 30

1967—Police Chief Retires

Norfolk police chief Harold Anderson retired. The sixty-five-year-old Anderson, who served as chief for twelve years, was brought to the city in 1956 by City Manager Tommy Maxwell, who worked with Anderson in Kansas City, Missouri. Anderson, a veteran of World War II and the Kansas City Police Department, brought a set of goals to the Norfolk force that were accomplished by the time he retired. Among the advances that occurred under Anderson's tenure were an increased salary for policemen, modernizing patrol car communications, opportunities for education and training and a forty-hour workweek. Under Anderson's term, the first black officer was promoted to sergeant.

MAY

May 1

1958—Inaugural Fishing Tourney Debuts at Ocean View

Virginia governor J. Lindsay Almond cast the first line into the Chesapeake Bay at Ocean View to begin the first- ever Virginia Salt Water Fishing Tournament. The event began with a luncheon at the Nansemond Hotel, which drew one hundred anglers. The tournament ran through November 1 and offered trophies for the largest catch of white marlin, croaker, spot, speckled trout, gray trout, tautog, red drum, black drum, bluefish, flounder and white perch. The catches needed to come from the Atlantic Ocean off Virginia, the Chesapeake Bay in Virginia and its bays and tributaries east of the fall line.

May 2

2009—Lioness Zola Delivers Four Cubs

The premiere lioness at the Virginia Zoo gave birth to a litter of four cubs. Zola made headlines two years earlier when she gave birth to a male and a female cub, Granby and Neka. It was the first large carnivore birth at the zoo in thirty-five years. Zola and cubs were to remain out of the public eye in order to bond as a family and share some special together time. Mramba was the father of both of Zola's litters.

May 3

1959—Boater Falls From Vessel and Loses Life

A weekend boating outing turned deadly when teenager Charles Dashiell lost his balance and fell from the craft on which he was riding after the boat was caught in the wake of another vessel. Dashiell managed to swim to safety, but the captain of the boat on which he had been riding did not experience the same good fortune. Thirty-eight-year-old Hilbert Tiberi was operating the boat on which Dashiell was a passenger, and after he ended up in the water, Tiberi made a sharp turn of the vessel, which caused him to also fall overboard. Tiberi drowned one hundred yards from shore.

May 4

1927—Ten Air Fatalties Cause Investigation

A board of inquiry assembled following the fourth plane crash in the Hampton Roads area involving naval aviators within a two-week period. The probe was called the day after two navy pilots perished when the seaplane in which they were flying went out of control and crashed near the Norfolk municipal pier. On April 22, two naval pilots crashed during a training flight. Three days later, two pilots lost their lives near Langley Field practicing for the New York to Paris nonstop flight, and four naval aviators were killed when their aircraft was struck by lightning over Hampton Roads on April 29.

May 5

2006—Mayor and Governor Lobby for Ford Plant

Virginia governor Tim Kaine and Norfolk mayor Paul Fraim met with three executives at Ford headquarters in Dearborn, Michigan. At stake was the fate of the Norfolk Ford assembly plant, which was scheduled to close in 2008. During the seventy-minute meeting held in a conference room at the company's product development center, a Ford official said while workers at the Norfolk plant were some of the "best workers in the world," she hoped that Virginia officials would not misspeak and give the plant's 2,400 employees false hopes that the facility would remain open.

May 6

1936—East Main Street Section of City Exposed

A nineteen-member grand jury requested an investigation of "appalling vice conditions" within the city. The East Main Street section was especially noted as a hotbed of "white slavery, the traffic of narcotics and the sale of liquor." The written statement that was issued urged the court to petition the city and state to aid federal authorities in alleviating the deplorable conditions.

May 7

1974—Howell Becomes First Woman to Serve on City Council

Elizabeth "Betty" McCarty Howell, wife of former Virginia lieutenant governor Henry Howell, made political history when she became the first woman elected to serve on the Norfolk City Council. Howell admitted that her name helped her gain her seat, but she also said that women at the polls expressed that it was time a woman was elected to sit on the city council. The Portsmouth native proved a popular representative and served from her election in 1974 until retiring in 1992.

May 8

1900—Extra! Newspapers Sold by Hawkers to Be Banned on Sunday

Norfolk's Select Council passed an ordinance expressing opposition of selling newspapers on Sunday by means of newsboys on the street. Current law forbade the "hawking" of papers by criers within a block of churches, but it was said the ordinance was not enforced. The motion came at the recommendation of a group of local preachers, who were to present their case before the Ordinance Committee of the city. The suggested ordinance did not ban Sunday sales of newspapers, just sales by overtly visible and audible means.

These boys sold newspapers on Norfolk streets. *Photo by Lewis Wickes Hine, Library of Congress.*

May 9

1862—President Comes Ashore

President Abraham Lincoln boarded the tug *Lioness* at Fort Monroe, traveled across Chesapeake Bay and came ashore at Ocean View in a small six-oared landing vessel. The Confederate cavalry attempted to turn back the president and opened fire from the beach. Lincoln's trip helped him formulate plans for an amphibious assault on Norfolk, which he shared with General John E. Wool after returning to the peninsula. Troops from Fort Monroe set out for the city at midnight and landed six thousand troops the next day at Willoughby Spit. Mayor William Lamb surrendered the city.

May 10

1976—Basketball Squires Shut Down by League

The troubled Virginia Squires team of the American Basketball Association was formally shut down by the league for inability to pay its debts. On this day, the franchise did not meet a 5:00 p.m. deadline to pay the ABA $100,000. Team manager, Jack Ankerson, said from the team's Norfolk office that he believed the owners would try to keep the team afloat. The Squires franchise was owned by approximately one hundred stockholders, including Van Cunningham, one of the founders of Norfolk-based Stewart Sandwiches, Inc.

May 11

1821—Navy Men Duel

A duel took place on this day between Lieutenant James Alexander Perry and Midshipman Sanders. Perry, the brother of U.S. Navy commodore Oliver Hazard Perry who gained a reputation as the "Hero of Lake Erie" for his actions fighting the British during the War of 1812, was seriously wounded in the throat during the altercation.

May 12

1963—Students Recognize and Support Birmingham Marchers

In a march organized by the NAACP and the Student Non-Violent Coordinating Committee, a group of high school and college students from Booker T. Washington High School, Old Dominion College and the Norfolk Division of Virginia State College showed support for civil rights marchers in Birmingham, Alabama. Peaceful demonstrators in that city, thought to be one of the most racially divided cities in the nation, were met with water hoses and police dogs. The Norfolk "sympathy marchers" walked from Brambleton Avenue, down Granby Street to Plume Street and up the other side of Granby.

May 13

1894—Presidential Hunting Party Transfers Tenders

President Grover Cleveland and members of his cabinet arrived in the city aboard the lighthouse tender *Maple* at 11:00 a.m. Cleveland and his entourage transferred to the tender *Violet* and headed to the Currituck Sound in North Carolina to spend three days hunting snipe. During his presidency, Cleveland made several trips between Washington and Currituck and Dare Counties in order to fish and hunt. Norfolk was often an important stopping-over point on his trips south and back. On this trip, Cleveland was scheduled to return to Washington after a week. Mrs. Cleveland took advantage of her husband's absence to take their daughters to visit their grandmother, her mother, Mrs. Folsom.

May 14

1927—British Group Breakfasts at Monticello Hotel

A group of delegates from the Federation of British Industries, the Chamber of Shipping of the United Kingdom, the British Chambers of Commerce and the Association of Chambers of Commerce of the Irish Free State were wrapping up a two-day, three-night visit in the city as part of an excursion to bolster commerce between Virginia and Great Britain. While in town, they lunched at the Norfolk Country Club and then visited the Tidewater Terminals, where they saw cotton bundled for export. The group also saw the coal piers of the Norfolk and Western Railway Company and witnessed coal loaded for export at the Virginian Railway Company. The Brits also toured other cities in Virginia and, traveling by train, made stops in Cincinnati, Louisville, Indianapolis, Chicago and Detroit.

May 15

1961—Petitions Circulate Against Public Money for Memorial

The organization Protectors of the Public Fund began circulating petitions against city money going toward the refurbishment of the century-old federal courthouse building in an effort to create a memorial to General Douglas MacArthur. The decorated general, whose mother was born in the Berkley section of Norfolk, desired his personal archives, memorabilia and his final resting place to be his mother's hometown. The Protectors of the Public Fund, with one hundred members, was organized by Constance F. Griffin, wife of a retired navy man. The goal of the group was to collect ten thousand signatures supporting its cause.

May 16

1970—Local Brunette Crowned Miss USA

Norfolk's Debbie Shelton, reigning Miss Virginia, was crowned Miss USA at a pageant in Miami Beach. The five-foot-eight, twenty-one-year-old student at Old Dominion University was the daughter of a Norfolk dentist. Earlier in the week, photographers covering the pageant named the green-eyed Shelton Miss Pixable for her ease in front of the camera. Shelton wore a modified navy uniform for her state outfit. It was the second year in a row that Miss Virginia had been awarded the Miss USA crown.

After becoming Miss Virginia, Norfolk's Debbie Shelton clenched the title of Miss USA. *Courtesy and © Miss Universe L.P., LLLP.*

May 17

1904—Ferry and Tug Collide

The passenger ferry the *City of Portsmouth* was on a morning route between the sister cities when it was brushed by the tug *Germania* of the Old Dominion Line. After receiving a warning, the passengers made for the life belts. The collision caused considerable concern, but the ferry, which was three hundred yards from docking, landed all its passengers safely. It was reported that "cool heads kept down the impending panic." The harbor incident would be investigated.

May 18

1832—St. Paul's Church Officially Consecrated

A 1739 structure, originally known as the Borough Church, was officially consecrated as St. Paul's Episcopal Church. The building withstood the shelling of the city during the Revolutionary War and even took a ball in the wall. The piece of ordnance eventually fell out but was later replaced and continues to draw the curious visitor. Following the war, divisions took place within the congregation, and after the founding of Christ Church in Ghent, the Borough Church building was loaned to white and black Baptist congregations. A generation later, Episcopalians repaired and brought back the original building that is still known as St. Paul's.

St. Paul's Episcopal Church began as the Borough Church in 1739. It is an iconic symbol of the city. *Library of Congress.*

May 19

1915—Merchants Meet in City

The Retail Merchants' Association of Virginia held its eleventh annual convention in Norfolk, with most sessions at the Monticello Hotel. All merchants in the state were welcome at the three-day meeting even if they were not association members. The Norfolk association members worked as hosts and offered a tour of the harbor to attending delegates. They also sponsored a theater party at the Academy of Music. Salem, Virginia's C.B. Strickler gave a presentation titled, "Boosting the Home Town: How Salem Did It."

May 20

2002—Former Mayor and Esteemed Leader Passes

Roy B. Martin Jr., who served as Norfolk's mayor during the revolutionary 1960s and '70s, died at his home after succumbing to cancer. He became the youngest representative on city council when Mayor Fred Duckworth appointed him as councilman in 1953. Six years later, Martin boldly voted against closing city schools during the massive resistance movement, the lone councilman to do so. He was known as the "bricks and mortar mayor," and during his tenure lasting additions to the city including Scope, the Chrysler Museum and the MacArthur Memorial came to fruition. After retiring from politics, he continued to lead and support the city he loved.

May 21

1964—Pink Pigeons Perplex Populace

Several reported sightings of pigeons pink in color near the downtown post office caused a cascade of conversation as to the origin of the bright birds. After an article about the avian accounts appeared in the *Ledger Star*, the perplexing pigeon puzzle was solved. It turned out that Morris Berger, who worked at a service station, was the cause of the colorful bird. He had trapped two pigeons and painted them pink believing it would "cause some comment." His earlier attempts to garner attention with a blue pigeon and a green pigeon failed.

May 22

1980—Sail-Powered Tug Becomes Reality

The *Norfolk Rebel* was christened on this day. The vessel, a sail-assisted tugboat, was the brainchild of marina owner Captain Lane Briggs. Harnessing the power of the wind increased the tug's speed and saved on the use of diesel fuel. Briggs sought to use the *Norfolk Rebel* for traditional towing operations, salvage duties and some commercial fishing. Mayor Vincent Thomas and a crowd of onlookers were on hand for the ceremony. In 2009, the group Friends of the *Norfolk Rebel* was established to aid in maintaining the historic ship.

May 23

1921—Lightning Strikes Church

During a severe electrical storm, a bolt of lightning hit the cupola of St. Luke's Episcopal Church on Granby Street, igniting it and causing the interior to catch fire and the entire building to burn completely. It was the second time within seven years that the building, described as magnificent, had been struck by lightning. Half a dozen fires were recorded in Norfolk, and storm damage was also reported in Hampton and Newport News. Instead of rebuilding downtown, the parish of St. Luke's merged with Christ Church, on the corner of Olney Road and Stockley Gardens, and is now known as Christ and St. Lukes.

May 24

2000—City's Ugliest Building Comes Down

Demolition began on the Jones Cold Storage facility, a waterfront industrial building that represented Norfolk's past. The six-story white concrete structure on East Water Street, near Harbor Park, had been described as "Norfolk's ugliest building" and was condemned by city officials. Almost all of the rubble from the 1920s graffiti-adorned structure would be recycled and used in construction projects around Tidewater.

May 25

1895—Play Ball! Norfolk Baseball Season Ready to Begin

The Norfolk Baseball Club had a morning and evening practice in preparation for the opening of the season. As many as three hundred fans came out to witness the new talent brought to the local club. The experienced players ranged in age from nineteen to twenty-nine. Fourteen men participated in the practices, and an additional two players, both pitchers, would arrive the following day. Although the fellows were a little stiff, some optimistic onlookers thought the club looked like pennant winners.

May 26

1922—City Represented In State Capital

Thousands of Norfolkians were on hand for Norfolk Day in Richmond to view the Virginia Historical Pageant. A group from Norfolk participated in the pageant in a segment entitled "The Commissioning of the Virginia," which reflected on actions during the "late unpleasantness." A parade was held in the morning, with several Norfolk interests noted. One float depicted the burning of Norfolk by the British in 1776. Boy Scouts from the city also participated in the parade. Special trains were arranged to carry citizens to the capital.

May 27

1968—Submarine Does Not Return

Wives and family members braved a late-spring nor'easter to await the return of their loved ones aboard of the nuclear submarine USS *Scorpion* at Pier 22 at the Norfolk Naval Base. The *Scorpion* was scheduled to return following a three-month deployment in the Mediterranean. Ninety-nine crewmen were aboard when the Skipjack-class submarine left Norfolk on February 15. Officials grew wary when the vessel did not make radio contact on the scheduled day of arrival. At 3:15 p.m., two and a half hours after the planned arrival time of the *Scorpion*, the navy issued a message to bases up and down the coast that the *Scorpion* was missing. Later in the year, parts of the vessel were located on the ocean floor 450 miles off the Azores. After information about the sub's disappearance was declassified and made available through the Freedom of Information Act, some believe the sub was sunk by a Russian torpedo.

May 28

1900—Many Visit City to View Eclipse

Norfolk was full of visitors, including faculty members from several colleges with telescopes in tow, to view the total eclipse of the sun at 8:54 a.m. Thousands viewed the spectacle from the piers of Hampton Roads. The Pennsylvania Railroad arranged a special rail excursion from Philadelphia to Norfolk. The train departed the City of Brotherly Love at 8:55 p.m. the night before. Sleeper cars were available. Stops were made in Chester, Pennsylvania, and Wilmington, Delaware, to pick up additional passengers interested in taking in the celestial event. At Cape Charles, the excursionists boarded a prearranged steamer on which a special breakfast was available for just seventy-five cents. President McKinley viewed the skies from the *Dolphin* near Lamberts Point. The cloudless sky gave the spectators perfect conditions to view the eclipse.

May 29

1906—First Wireless Message from Norfolk Received by Roosevelt

The first wireless transmission from the city was sent from the newly completed DeForest Station atop the Bank of Commerce building and was received on the presidential yacht *Mayflower*. President Theodore Roosevelt was en route to Portsmouth to deliver a Memorial Day address to a group of servicemen. Along with the chief executive were Mrs. Roosevelt, the first lady's sister and the two Roosevelt children. The *Mayflower* was near Kettle Bottom Shoals in the Potomac River when the message was received.

May 30

1939—Memorial Day Parade Draws Crowds

The city's annual Memorial Day Parade was an especially festive one with several marching units, including veteran and active military groups, Red Cross nurses, Boy Scouts, the American Legion Drum and Bugle Corps and the Maury High School Marching Band. While Norfolk threw an impressive parade, proper credit should be noted here that the sister city by the sea, Portsmouth, has the distinction of having the nation's longest continuously held Memorial Day Parade, which began in 1884.

Memorial Day Parade on Granby Street. *Photo by Charles Borjes, courtesy Sargeant Memorial Collection, Norfolk Public Library.*

May 31

1923—Rum Money Comes Ashore

The master of the British steam yacht *Istar* visited a Norfolk bank in order to exchange $250,000 for British currency. The yacht, which was at anchor fifteen miles off the Virginia coast, had been under close surveillance by the Coast Guard, which suspected the *Istar* to be a rumrunner. While in Norfolk, the owner, who came ashore in a yawl, reported that he was hoping to make one more successful trip in order to retire with profits of $1 million. The captain made it clear that the ship had never brought liquor within fifteen miles of the American coast.

JUNE

June 1

1951—Final Reunion of Veterans Underway

The sixty-first and final reunion of members of the United Confederate Veterans took place in the city and was headquartered at the Monticello Hotel. Only twelve known Confederate veterans were living at this time, and only three—centenarians all—attended this last gathering. The men who made the trip were 104-year-old John Salling from Slant, Virginia; 105-year-old William D. Townsend of Olla, Louisiana; and 105-year-old William Joshua Bush of Fitzgerald, Georgia.

June 2

1835—Vessel Begins Run Between Norfolk and Charleston

The steamship *South Carolina*, sailing under Captain Rollins, began regular service between Norfolk and Charleston, and a summer schedule was published. The new vessel was constructed of quality materials and built to rival any similar vessel in the United States. With its fifteen-horsepower engine, it was expected that the *South Carolina* would make the trip between the two port cities in forty hours and "scarcely, if ever, [be] out of sight of land." The vessel *Dolphin* also provided summer passenger service between Norfolk and Charleston.

June 3

1872—New Hotel Receives First Guests at Sewell's Point

A new hostelry billed as a "First Class Watering Place on the Seaside" opened for business. Rooms would be available at the Vu de L'eau Hotel for three dollars a day or thirty-five dollars for a two-week stay, and a one-month visit could be had for sixty dollars. The advertisement announcing the opening promised "splendid fishing, fine boating, salt water bathing, shaded groves, billiards, ten pins, music and every luxury of the sea and land." Special railway rates were available to hotel guests, and steamers from Norfolk and Portsmouth made frequent runs.

June 4

2002—City to Purchase Motel at Major Intersection

Norfolk City Council voted to purchase the old Red Roof Inn hotel at the corner of Virginia Beach Boulevard and Tidewater Drive. The price tag for the troubled building was just over $1 million, and city officials planned to spend an additional $150,000 to tear it down. The hotel had a sketchy past. In 1999, known then as Town Point Hotel, it was declared a "drug blight." The four-and-a-half-acre site remains undeveloped.

June 5

1983—Waterside Merchants Cited for Blue Law Violation

Sixteen merchants at the brand-new downtown shopping pavilion and festival site, Waterside, were cited for violating the state's blue laws that prohibited operating on Sundays. Norfolk City Council moved quickly and two days later passed legislation declaring that the $13.5 million attraction was city property as well as a festival site, which would exempt Waterside businesses from the state law. Virginia attorney general Gerald Baliles backed the council's decision. "Without the city's active participation and public investment, the project would not have come into existence at all," he said.

June 6

1968—Ground Broken for Downtown Arena

Groundbreaking took place on what was then called the Norfolk Cultural and Convention Center but would later be known as Scope. The highly recognizable concrete dome arena was part of the downtown revitalization following World War II. The eleven-thousand-seat arena, which opened in November 1971, was designed by Norfolk architects Williams and Tazewell and Associates. It was one of the home courts for the Virginia Squires basketball team, and Norfolk boxer Pernell "Sweet Pea" Whittaker fought several bouts there. It is currently the home venue for the Admirals hockey team. Scope has hosted evangelist Billy Graham, venerable vocalist Frank Sinatra, British rockers the Rolling Stones and pop culture sensation Justin Bieber.

June 7

1975—Search Resumes for Missing Boaters

Five helicopters, two Coast Guard patrol boats and members of the Norfolk and Virginia Beach police departments continued their search for nine individuals who were on the charter fishing boat *Dixie Lee II* the day before when a fourteen-foot wave knocked the vessel to its side. Fourteen people were rescued immediately following the incident by the party boat *Joyce Lee*. Five were confirmed drowned. Although the weather was reported as beautiful when the *Dixie Lee II* left the dock, a fast-moving storm with wind gusts as high as ninety-six miles per hour caused the forty-two-foot boat to capsize five miles north of the city and three miles east of the Hampton Roads Bridge Tunnel.

June 8

1970—Noted Liner Docked

On this day, it was announced that the SS *United States*, the ocean liner that held the record for the fastest transatlantic crossing, would be retired and docked at Norfolk International Terminals. In its heyday, the ship made four hundred voyages between the United States and Europe carrying tens of thousands of passengers, including notable royals, politicians and celebrities. The cost of storing the eighteen-year-old luxury liner would be $9,000 a year, paid by the United States Lines. The *United States* had become unprofitable to operate because of crew salaries and increased competition from airlines. Since 1996, the ship has been docked in Philadelphia.

June 9

2003—Industrial Leak Sends Nine to Area Hosptials

A HAZMAT team responded after a truck driver detected the smell of chemicals in a shipping container he had just delivered to Norfolk Industrial Park. The Norfolk Warehouse Distribution Centers was evacuated, and nine individuals were treated and released from local hospitals. Those affected had been exposed to a toxic industrial chemical called epichlorohydrin. Officials said that those exposed did not lose consciousness and were able to take decontamination showers at the Industrial Park, reducing the risk of permanent damage. It was determined that the leak was not active, and a private firm was brought in for cleanup.

June 10

1896—Orphanage and School Begun

Groundbreaking took place for a new school and orphanage on Chapel, Mariner and Fenchurch Streets. The new three-story structures, built under the auspices of the Sisters of Charity, would measure fifty by one hundred feet and would be constructed of brick and trimmed in buff-colored stone. Frank May was awarded the contract with a bid of $23,500. Two older buildings were removed in order to make room for the new edifices, which were said to be "a fine improvement to that section of the city." Construction was expected to be completed by mid-September.

June 11

1968—Noted Lawyer Elected to City Council, Breaks Ground

Norfolk attorney Joseph A. Jordan Jr. was elected to the Norfolk City Council and, in doing so, became the first black representative on that government body. He rose to the office of vice-mayor in 1972. A city native and veteran of World War II, Jordan argued several civil rights cases. He represented Evelyn Butts in a 1963 lawsuit filed to have state poll taxes removed. The case was defeated locally and on the state level several times before being heard in the U.S. Supreme Court in March 1966. Jordan also envisioned and raised funds for a memorial to Martin Luther King Jr. in Norfolk. He is remembered by the author of this book for his wise and friendly demeanor displayed at Career Day at Madison Elementary School.

June 12

1934—City Gets Fourth Liquor Store

The Virginia Alcohol Beverage Control Board in Richmond announced plans for a new state-controlled liquor store at 106 West Princess Anne Road that was expected to open in ten days. Another ABC store on Colley Avenue was expected to open soon as well. The Princess Anne Road store would be the fourth established in the city since the repeal of Prohibition on December 5, 1933. Additional stores were already in operation at 101 West Main Street and on Church Street.

June 13

1967—Mayor Suggests Merger

A letter penned by Norfolk mayor Roy B. Martin Jr. and sent to Virginia Beach mayor Frank A. Dusch was made public following a regular meeting of the Norfolk City Council. In the letter, Martin proposed forming a twelve-member committee to take a look at the possibility of the two cities merging. Each municipality would provide six members to the panel. Earlier in the week, Virginia Beach's Sidney A. Kellam spoke before the Virginia Beach City Council urging officials to prevent the loss of any Virginia Beach land to Norfolk.

June 14

1900—Benefit Recital Given for Blind Musician

A concert was given by the students of the Norfolk Conservatory of Music to benefit J.H. Mack, who, although blind, was an accomplished musician living in the city. Mack, who played both the flute and oboe, was often seen on Main Street and was known for the "sweet piping he dispenses." The 8:30 p.m. concert took place in Montefiore Hall and featured several vocal selections in the form of solos and quartets. Mr. Mack participated too, playing an original composition. It was reported that the event was "largely attended and much enjoyed."

June 15

1920—Committee Declines to Aid Richmond in Transportation Venture

A special committee made up of Norfolk interests met and decided that instead of joining in on a plan to initiate a direct steamship line between Richmond and New York City, it would create its own line with the Big Apple. It was reported that Norfolk's not wanting to collaborate in the cooperative venture added "spirit and determination" to the effort and galvanized Richmonders. The following day, J. Scott Parrish, chairman of the Richmond Chamber of Commerce Transportation Committee, said service would begin as soon as boats could be procured. It was believed Norfolk's refusal to participate would benefit the capital city overall.

June 16

2007—Young Animal Lover Remembered

On this day, the memory of Jackson Clarke Fox was honored with the dedication of bronze statues at the Virginia Zoo. Friends and family raised over $50,000 to purchase the sculptures as a way to remember the thirteen-year-old Boy Scout who perished in a car crash near his home in Franklin, Virginia, along with two other scouts and a scout leader. Fox loved animals and had attended a weeklong camp at the zoo two years in a row. The Franklin teen hoped to attend Virginia Tech, his father's alma mater, and to become a veterinarian.

June 17

1897—Yachters Have Pleasant Day

On this day, a special party was given by society man Harry B. Goodridge. Several friends, including out-of-town guests from Baltimore, were invited on a yachting excursion on Goodrich's sloop, *Vivian*. The group met at the Willoughby Club at Ocean View beach, the women arriving in the morning and the men joining them later in the afternoon. At 4:00 p.m., the party set out for a sail to the Capes.

June 18

1961—Hall of Famer and Sack Record Holder Born

Bruce Smith was born in the city this day. Smith played high school football at Booker T. Washington and college ball at Virginia Tech,

Norfolk-born Bruce Smith had a stellar football career. *Digital Library and Archives, University Libraries, Virginia Tech, http://spec.lib.vt.edu/imagebase/04VT/VisCom/screen/6UR030611TRAY1SLOT34.jpg .*

where he was known as the "Sack Man." While in Blacksburg, Smith earned record accolades for his achievements. He was the first pick in the 1985 season, claimed by the Buffalo Bills. He later played as a free agent for the Washington Redskins, where he reached a career record of over two hundred quarterback sacks. Smith was enshrined in the National Football Hall of Fame in 2009 in his first year of eligibility.

June 19

1942—Mosquito Group Visits Wartime Norfolk

The Eastern Association of Mosquito Workers made an inspection visit to the city, and during their stay, the group members toured Boush Creek, a salt marsh that had reduced mosquitos by the creation of ditches. The visitors also viewed Mason Creek. Much of the day was spent at the General Booth Farm, a working farm for minor offenders. Both the Bureau of Mosquito Control and the prison farm were under the Department of Public Welfare. The group was able to see firsthand the temporary housing that was "muchrooming [*sic*] overnight for the defense workers."

June 20

1980—Elderly Woman Shoots from Balcony

Police responded to a call of someone shooting at children and found an elderly woman firing randomly from her apartment. She did not respond when police knocked on her door, but as they were leaving, she fired a shot through the door. The woman then went to her back porch and pointed a gun at an officer. After refusing orders to drop the weapon, the officer responded with a single fatal shot.

June 21

2006—School Board Votes for Healthy Vending

In an effort to follow guidelines of the Virginia Action for Healthy Kids, the Norfolk School Board moved to improve items available for sale in school vending machines. More options for juice and milk would replace the selection of sodas and carbonated and caffeinated beverages. The healthier options would become available after a five-year contract with Mid-Atlantic Coca-Cola Bottling Company expired. The new offerings would be available for the 2007 school year in 175 vending machines, and 16 machines already offered healthier selections.

June 22

1813—Battle of Craney Island Turns Back Brits

A large military presence had been amassing in the city for ten months in order to defend Norfolk from an ever-growing British threat. Eighteen British ships of war under the command of General Cockburn assembled in February and March just inside the mouth of the Chesapeake Bay. Cockburn had grand plans that included blockading the mouth of the bay, seizing ships, scouting the shoreline and invading the city. Some of Norfolk's citizens at this time chose to visit relatives in the country. In preparation, General Robert B. Taylor sank ships in the Elizabeth River and fortified Craney Island in the Elizabeth River and Old Point Comfort at the entrance to Hampton Roads. Fewer than eight hundred men on Craney Island, along with a handful of Federal gunboats, turned back a much-larger British contingent under a barrage of gunfire.

June 23

1928—Nansemond Hotel Opens at Ocean View

The three-story bay-front Nansemond Hotel began receiving visitors. Billed as "A Bit of Old Spain," and "modern in every detail," the building featured Moorish furnishings and accents inside and out. Arched windows, tile floors, wrought-iron embellishments and woven rugs set the resort apart from others of that time. Local architect Bernard Spigel designed the hostelry for Mr. and Mrs. C.A. Baker, who ran a smaller "Nansemond" from their private home, which they had enlarged to take in guests. In 1942, the hotel served as headquarters of the commander of Amphibious Force of the U.S. Atlantic Fleet.

The Nansemond Hotel at Ocean View opened for business in 1928. *Photo by Charles Borjes, courtesy Sargeant Memorial Collection, Norfolk Public Library.*

June 24

1996—Rocker Hynde Rings in PETA's New Digs

Chrissy Hynde, lead singer for the band the Pretenders, performed at the welcoming ceremony for the organization People for Ethical Treatment of Animals (PETA), which was moving into a new Norfolk headquarters. Hynde quipped, "They say that Virginia is for lovers, but we say Virginia is for animal lovers." Main offices were scheduled to start business July 1. Reasons for moving the number-one animal rights group to Norfolk were that it was an easier place to get around in and a less expensive place to live in than the Washington, D.C. area.

June 25

1999—Ferry Service to Hampton Begins

A new ferry service between downtown Norfolk and downtown Hampton began aboard the ship *Zephyr*. Up to 140 passengers could pay ten dollars for one of six daily round trips between the two cities. Additional trips were added on Friday and Saturday nights. The ninety-foot *Zephyr* made the twelve-mile trip in just forty-five minutes. It was hoped that the ferry would be popular with commuters and sightseers. The *Zephyr*'s start date was originally June 18 but had to be rescheduled in order to make necessary repairs to its propeller.

June 26

1900—Coatless Lad Denied Damages

On this day H. Garrett Smith was denied damage claims he made for two thousand dollars. The incident in question stemmed from an event aboard the steamer *Louise*. Smith entered a saloon aboard the ship in just an "outing shirt" and no coat. He was asked by the ship's purser to comply with the ship's regulations and move to a lower deck where his dress would be acceptable. Smith believed, as a first-class ticket holder, he could come and go in first-class areas of the ship.

June 27

1979—Ocean View's Rocket Won't Go Down

The eighty-year-old wooden roller coaster the Rocket, centerpiece of Ocean View Amusement Park, which closed eight months earlier, withstood two rounds of dynamite blasts in an attempt to bring it down. Crews from ABC were on site to film the coaster exploding for a made-for-TV movie *Death of Ocean View Park*. Seventy-six sticks of dynamite and two hundred gallons of gasoline were used in the first try, and twice the amount of dynamite—three and a half cases—was used in the second ill-fated attempt. Two days later, the Rocket was brought down in a third explosion. *Death at Ocean View Park* starred Mike Connors and Martin Landau.

June 28

1937—Act Approved for Commemorative Coin

The Seventy-fifth Congress authorized the minting of a silver half-dollar to mark both the 300th anniversary of the Norfolk land grant as well as the 250th anniversary of the founding of the Borough of Norfolk. The number produced was not to exceed twenty-five thousand, and they were to be dated 1936 regardless of the year in which they were struck. Just under seventeen thousand were produced at the Philadelphia Mint. The half-dollar was designed by artist William Marks Simpson. The front featured a sailing ship, a plow and three shocks of grain and the words *Et Terra Mare Divitiae Tuae* (which translates to "by land and sea thy riches are") and the word *Crescas* (which means "thou shalt grow"). A likeness of the Norfolk mace and 1636 are on the coin's reverse.

June 29

1978—Chief Executive Fishes Off Virginia Coast on Gannet

President Jimmy Carter, wife Roslyn and daughter Amy were guests of Norfolk attorney Pete Decker Jr. on his fifty-five-foot sport fishing vessel

President Jimmy Carter enjoyed catching dolphin with Pete Decker in 1978 and returned to go bluefishing in 1979. *Photo courtesy Jimmy Carter Library and Museum.*

Gannet. The first family was joined by Cecil Andrus, secretary of the Department of the Interior. The party flew from Washington via helicopter and fished for dolphin off the Virginia coast. Newspapers ran a photo of the president holding up two of the three tuna caught. It was reported of the three fish boated, Amy's thirty-pounder was the largest.

June 30

1938—Federal Money Allotted for Azaela Gardens

The Works Progress Administration (WPA), one of President Franklin D. Roosevelt's programs that put Americans to work on improvement projects around the country, granted $76,278 for the building of a formal garden in Norfolk. The project, called Azalea Gardens, was conceived by city manager Thomas P. Thompson. He believed azaleas would thrive in the area's unique environment and a planned garden would attract visitors to the city. Because most of the male labor was busy with other projects, two hundred black women and twenty black men were employed to clear the swampy terrain. By the following spring, over four thousand azaleas were planted. The site is now known as Norfolk Botanical Garden, and in 2009, a special WPA Memorial Garden was unveiled to pay tribute to those who worked long, hard hours to make such a lasting living legacy.

JULY

July 1

1865—Federal Soldiers Shake Down Servants

Two black men employed by the Atlantic Hotel were stopped by Federal soldiers and made to empty the contents of their pockets. The incident took place around 11:00 p.m. at the corner of Queen and Monroe Streets. Jefferson Davis, who once was the body servant of Confederate general Joseph Eggleston Johnston, was robbed of two dollars and fifty cents. Thomas Glover surrendered a pistol. Following the shakedown, the soldiers "cursed their victims heartily" and then told the men to "track."

July 2

1990—Crews Work to Clean Oil Spill and Protect Beaches

Following the collision of two cargo vessels in the Chesapeake Bay, teams from the Coast Guard, navy and a private contractor worked to control a fuel spill estimated at thirty thousand gallons. The spill was concentrated in the shipping channel, and if it reached shore, it was most likely to do so at Ocean View. The collision occurred the night before during a thunderstorm when the seagoing *Columbus America* lost its fuel after striking the harbor-bound *Neptune Jade.* It was the worst such spill in over a decade. The shipping channel was closed for four hours during the cleanup. The Chesapeake Bay Foundation expressed concern that if the oil sank to the bottom of the bay, it would kill crab larvae.

July 3

2003—Holland America to Cruise from Norfolk

Norfolk mayor Paul Fraim announced that the Holland America Line had agreed to make Norfolk the port for its cruise ship *Maasdam*. Officials thought Norfolk was a fine central port with millions of potential customers/cruisers within driving distance. Holland America agreed to sixteen departures from the city between January and April and then again from October to December. The city would benefit economically by the increase in retail and restaurant sales and hotel bookings. The first cruise was sold out and departed the city on January 20, 2004.

July 4

1884—Regatta Held While City in Midsummer Holiday

A large crowd gathered for the first-ever State Regatta of the Virginia Association of Amateur Oarsmen. The first race of the day featured three crews, the Columbias and the Potomacs from our nation's capital and the Elizabeths from Norfolk's sister city, Portsmouth. The event was a four-oared shell race in which four rowers with one oar a piece (two starboard and two port) raced a mile and a half. The second race was a four-oared gig race between Petersburg's Cockade and Appomattox crews and Norfolk's Gymnasium crew. The Norfolk rowers, in their first regatta competition, won by seven lengths. It was reported that following the victory, townsfolk were "wild with delight."

July 5

1875—Steamer Strikes Same Near Sewell's Point

The steamer *Lumberman* carrying eighteen passengers was struck by the vessel *Isaac Bell* near Sewell's Point. The ship, returning from Fort Monroe, sank in fifty feet of water. Five of the *Lumberman*'s passengers were rescued in three boats launched from the *Isaac Bell*. Ten were drowned, and by the following day, only three bodies had been recovered, while boats dragged the bottom for others. The tragedy caused a sensation in the city, and rumors circulated freely as to the cause of the incident. After testimony was given, it was determined that a navigation error on the part of the captain of the *Lumberman* caused the collision.

July 6

1994—Student Stabs Calculus Instructor

A part-time freshman student at Old Dominion University surprised his classmates, who numbered about two dozen, when he brandished a knife and stabbed his calculous professor in the shoulder. The attack was unprovoked. After the incident, the twenty-year-old waited for law enforcement to arrive. Campus police arrested him in the Batten Arts and Letters Building in the classroom where the violence took place. The student was charged with malicious wounding and terminated as an Old Dominion University student. The instructor was treated at Norfolk General Hospital and later released.

July 7

1900—Ice Prices at a Premium

A scarcity of ice, caused in part by broken machinery at a local ice plant, coincided with a spell of hot weather. In turn, some "box dealers" who bought in bulk to sell to retailers raised their fee to one cent and, in some cases, two cents a pound. The Norfolk Ice Delivery Company charged the regular price for its regular established customers—fifty cents per pound for less than one hundred pounds, forty cents a pound for between one hundred and two hundred pounds and thirty-five cents for deliveries of between two hundred and five hundred pounds. Part of the reason for the increase in price was that the "box men" resorted to purchasing their wholesale ice in Portsmouth.

July 8

1971—Mom and Youngsters Enjoy Country Club Pool

Newspapers across the United States ran an Associated Press wire story about a mother duck and her eight ducklings who had become regular guests at the Norfolk Yacht and Country Club pool. The hen and her brood had been showing up just around 11:00 a.m. each day for over a week. They apparently preferred the pool as opposed to the Lafayette River. After taking their morning dip, the ducks enjoyed relaxing poolside and taking in the river views.

July 9

1985—City Council Votes to Support Cousteau

By a six-to-one vote, Norfolk City Council backed a conditional approval of a proposed $24.7 million Cousteau Ocean Center to be built on the city's waterfront as part of its revitalization. Initial planning allowed for the issuance of bonds backed by taxpayers. The center would highlight the work of undersea explorer Jacques Yves Cousteau, who was expected to participate in a campaign to raise $5 million for the center. The planned facility would include state-of-the-art exhibits on underwater exploration and preserving the world's oceans.

July 10

1965—Norfolk Neptunes Look to Fill Roster

The Norfolk Neptunes, a football team of the new Continental League, held a two-day tryout session at Foreman Field in order to assemble a team for the upcoming season. Candidates were to bring their own shoes and gear and a note from their doctor. Those who made the cut would be housed in the Rogers Hall dormitory of Old Dominion College and would begin a three-week training session the day after the tryouts. The season opener was scheduled for August.

July 11

1926—Texas Visitor Nearly Drowns

A frightful scene unfolded when Mrs. C.F. Leroux found herself literally in over her head at Ocean View. Three men took part in the rescue of the visitor from Houston, Texas. The first to hear her call and attempt to pull Mrs. Leroux from the water was a medical student from Illinois, M.J. Prescor, but not being a strong swimmer, he was exhausted by the time he reached the victim. A sailor from the USS *Vestal*, Peter Roach, made an attempt but both he and Leroux were unconscious when they were pulled from the water near shore. They were revived by the use of a pulmotor, an early resuscitator, which was administered by Chief Petty Officer Miller from the naval base.

July 12

2011—President at Kimnach Ford Announces Closure

Jay Council Jr., president of Kimnach Ford, announced to employees on this day that the Virginia Beach Boulevard business would close at the end of the week. Kimnach, an established and well-known name in the Tidewater car business, was launched in 1956, although the roots of the company could be traced to the late 1930s. Many considered Kimnach's closing to be the end of an era. Following the staff meeting, signs were posted to inform customers of the upcoming closure.

July 13

1920—Peanut Men Wrap Up Meeting in City

The United Peanut Association of America, an organization made up of peanut growers, peanut shellers and crushers and others with interests in the peanut industry, was wrapping up its two-day inaugural convention in Norfolk. The gathering brought people from across the country. The first item on the agenda was initiating a protective tariff on peanuts that were being imported into the country. The following year, association members, along with noted inventor, scientist and biologist George Washington Carver, testified to a congressional committee as to the economic importance of the humble legume.

July 14

1901—Virginian Presented Sword

People of Norfolk honored a native son on this evening, presenting a sword to Major Littleton W.F. Walker of the U.S. Marine Corps. The low-key ceremony was held at the Academy of Music, where Norfolk mayor James G. Riddick introduced city leader and delegate to the Virginia Constitutional Convention Alfred P. Thom, who in turn presented the sword to Walker. It was reported that Walker shook hands with all in the audience. The bequest included a banquet dinner with the Norfolk Artillery Blues, a local long-standing militia organization.

July 15

1940—High Rock Park Dedicated

The new home stadium of the Norfolk Tars baseball team was dedicated in front of a crowd of thousands. The fans, packed in the wooden stands, watched the Tars lose to the Richmond Colts. One might think High Rock a silly name for a stadium in an area that was notably low and sandy. The price tag for the new stadium was $75,000. In 1944, High Rock Park sustained substantial damage during a fire. Dr. Eddie Meyers, owner of the Norfolk Tars, had the stadium rebuilt. The venue was later known as Meyers Field.

July 16

1912—Public Law Enacted Defining Stables and Regulating Poo

On this day, an ordinance was passed that defined stables within the city and made it illegal to "erect, alter or repair" one without a proper permit. In warm months, the floors of stables were to be treated daily with a disinfectant and weekly over the winter, and each day, manure was to be removed or placed in an appropriate bin by 9:00 a.m. Stables were defined as any structure that would shelter "one or more horses, mules, cows or cattle." Violators would be fined, and each day the stable was in noncompliance would be considered a separate offense.

July 17

1897—Roundtrip Tickets from Richmond to Norfolk Just One Dollar

As part of its summer Sunday excursions, the Norfolk and Western Railroad Line offered all-rail direct service to Norfolk and then on to Ocean View and Virginia Beach. The line touted its "new rails" and "slack ballasted track," which it claimed made for a ride that was "smooth and nice." The trains left Byrd Station in Richmond at 8:30 a.m. and picked up excursionists in Petersburg, Waverly and Suffolk. Return trains left Ocean View at 6:30 p.m., Virginia Beach at 7:00 p.m. and Norfolk at 7:30 p.m. Tickets were sold onboard.

July 18

2012—Changes at Ward's Corner

On this day, excavators of the Chesapeake-based Atlantic Coast Contractors worked to bring down buildings at Ward's Corner, originally an "uptown" shopping center at the corner of Granby Street and Little Creek Road. In its early days, Ward's Corner was billed as the "Times Square of the South." The building that was torn down was A.J. Gators sports bar. The demolition marked another step in the renewal process of Ward's Corner. Just over a year and a half later, a new Harris Teeter opened at that spot.

July 19

1917—Troops Guard Bridges

United States Navy Rear-Admiral A.C. Dillingham sent armed soldiers to guard both the Lafayette River Bridge and the Norfolk and Western Viaduct after receiving word that his lines of communication could be tampered with. An attempt to burn the viaduct was foiled. Reports had also been received that the Tanners Creek Bridge would be taken out. Transportation lines were to be kept open in order to move men and supplies between Norfolk and the new naval base at the former Jamestown Exposition Grounds, where three thousand were employed.

July 20

1932—Treasure Hunters Seek Gold and Jewels Off Virginia Capes

The treasure-hunting vessel *Salvor* was taking on supplies and preparing to leave Norfolk in search of sunken gold, silver and jewels. The expedition was led by Captain Harry L. Bowdoin, who brought along a diving suit, which he had worked on perfecting for a number of years. Bowdoin was seeking the sunken ship *Merida*, a former vessel of the Ward Line that came to rest at the bottom of the sea an estimated sixty-five miles off Cape Henry in May 1911 after colliding with the *Admiral Farragut*, a steamer of the United Fruit Company. The booty was valued somewhere between $4 and $6 million.

July 21

1960—Educational Leader Calcott Dies

On this day, Mrs. Mary Whitworth Calcott passed away in a Norfolk Hospital. A champion of education, she was the second woman to hold a seat on the Norfolk City School Board. She served from her appointment in 1927 to 1952. The Norfolk Cosmopolitan Club named Calcott Norfolk's First Citizen in 1945. Other accolades she was awarded were Mother of the Year in 1946 by the Golden Rule Foundation and Outstanding Woman Citizen of Norfolk in 1939 by the Business and Professional Woman's Club. She served on the Norfolk Commission on Higher Education and the board of Norfolk Polytechnic College, which later would become Norfolk State University. Incidentally, after her retirement from the school board in 1952, a new elementary school in the Bayview section of Norfolk was named in her honor. At the time of her death, Mrs. Calcott was eighty-nine years old.

July 22

1934—Greensboro Man Found Dead in Hotel Room

Robert Nathan Smith of Greensboro, North Carolina, and Dundee, Florida, was found dead in his hotel room after staff members forced their way into Smith's suite. Also in the room were letters, one of which contained a check for $3,000 made out to the order of Smith's wife, and two partially full liquor bottles and some poison. It was reported that Smith had between $8,000 and $10,000 in insurance policies in addition to the check. The following day, a coroner's inquest was requested.

July 23

1979—Piedmont Airlines Picks Up Abandoned Routes

Less than a week after United Air Lines dropped four daily round-trip flights between Norfolk and Atlanta, Piedmont Airlines took advantage of the opportunity and added flights to Atlanta, Georgia; Charleston, South Carolina; and New York City. A spokesman for Piedmont, Bill Howard, senior executive vice president, also announced that by the end of the year it would begin service between destinations in Florida. The news came at a morning meeting at Norfolk International Airport.

July 24

2013—Baby Giraffe Named

Over four thousand people participated in suggesting names for a new 150-pound, six-foot four-inch baby giraffe born on June 6 at the Virginia Zoo. The name Kellen was selected by zoo staff and social media users after a woman made the suggestion in memory of her son Kellen, who died from Sudden Infant Death Syndrome. Kellen is a Masai giraffe, the tallest land mammal. The other top vote-getting names were Patches, Zarafa, Mandela and Twiga.

July 25

1888—Secession to North Carolina Subject of Letter

Someone with the pen name Junius wrote a letter that was sent to the editor of the *Charlotte Observer* and was printed in the *Times Dispatch* a week or so later. In it, the author suggested that Norfolk should be annexed as part of North Carolina and pointed out a long association between the city and the

Tar Heel State. The writer also made mention that Norfolkians had a right to feel incensed due to the "hostile attitude shown towards it by the rest of the state and by the state government." Junius gave examples of Norfolk and the eastern portion of Virginia not receiving appointments to important committees and commissions even though one-third of the population of the state resided east of the state capital.

July 26

1890—City Woos Tennessee Newspaper Men

A group of Tennesseans took a side excursion from Bristol, on the Tennessee-Virginia border, to Norfolk, following the annual meeting of the Tennessee Press Association. The group was wowed by Norfolk's openness and noted that "a clever, more friendly and hospitable people cannot be found in any city." During their stay, they were greeted by members of the Business Men's Association and local pressmen and took a cruise to see "points of interest around the harbor." They stayed at the new Atlantic Hotel and were impressed by the clerk's "pleasure in answering questions" and how "all of the servants and waiters were on alert and responded promptly to every request." It was noted that "there is a fine opening at Norfolk for a modern progressive daily newspaper," and they regretted that their visit "was too brief."

July 27

1983—Detectives Meet in Norfolk to Share Notes on Preppy Bandits

A string of thefts of gold chains by young clean-cut thieves wearing designer clothing, including Jordache jeans, caused detectives from Norfolk, Chesapeake, Hampton and Virginia Beach to come together at Norfolk Police Headquarters to share information. A small gang, predominantly male, young, polite and well dressed, were preying on department stores and jewelry stores in malls on the south side and the peninsula. During some of the robberies, the thieves were able to steal gold chains and other jewelry worth $10,000.

July 28

1865—Scorcher in City

The city was experiencing a particularly hot spell, and on this day, the temperature in the shade was reported to be 107 degrees. The *Norfolk Post* confessed that "all ye that can lay back in the shade" in the environs "about Witch Duck and Ocean View, we envy you. Stay where you are, and enjoy it." The heat, which was described as intense, began three days earlier and made those in town "pant for a soft and gentle breeze." The temperature was taken on the thermometer at W.E. Lewis's Drug Store under the Atlantic Hotel on Main Street.

July 29

1940—President Tours Naval Base

After arriving in Hampton Roads aboard the presidential yacht *Potomac*, President Franklin D. Roosevelt was driven throughout the city as part of a

President Franklin D. Roosevelt touring the Norfolk Naval Base. *Photo by Charles Borjes, courtesy Sargeant Memorial Collection, Norfolk Public Library.*

defense inspection tour of the U.S. Naval Base. The chief executive was greeted by enthusiastic crowds as the automobile in which he was traveling made its way through Norfolk. Upon his arrival, Roosevelt was greeted by Rear Admiral Joseph Taussig and Congressman Colgate W. Darden. It was reported that Roosevelt was pleased with the work being done for the defense of the country.

July 30

1821—Children Ingest Hallucinogen

Three children, all under the age of six, consumed two or three seeds of the plant known as jimson weed or Jamestown weed (*Datura stramonium*). The plant is a strong deliriant and causes an increased pulse, dilated pupils, nausea and heightened mood followed by episodes of terror. The father of two of the children, Henry Murden, immediately summonsed Dr. Archer, who tended to the youngsters until the effects of the weed wore off. The children made a full recovery, but the doctor feared that had they ingested any more of the poison, the outcome would not have been as bright. A written account of the episode urged readers to become familiar with the plant to prevent another mishap.

July 31

1943—First Dance Held in New Municipal Auditorium

A new auditorium was completed and became a much-used venue for entertaining the wartime servicemen and women. The building was leased to the United Service Organization (USO). In addition to dances, concerts, sporting events and lectures were held there. Center Theater, which shared the building, was completed in January 1944. The structure has been refurbished and is now known as the Harrison Opera House.

AUGUST

August 1

1954—Train Service Between Petersburg and City Consolidated

Two scheduled Norfolk and Western passenger train trips between Norfolk and Petersburg, a morning route and an evening route, were discontinued. At a hearing of the State Corporation Commission, officials testified that four trips a day were not needed, and two would certainly meet the needs of the traveling public. No one spoke in opposition of the consolidation at the hearing. Travel between the two cities had decreased dramatically, and trimming the schedule would save Norfolk and Western close to $90,000 a year.

August 2

1976—Nancy Lieberman to Play at ODU

Women's basketball standout and Olympian Nancy Lieberman, who was just back from her trip to the Montreal Summer Olympics, where the U.S. women's basketball team earned a silver medal, told Old Dominion University coach Pam Parsons that she would play college ball at ODU. Lieberman would lead the team to two back-to-back Association of Intercollegiate Athletics for Women (AIAW) championships in 1979 and 1980. During her college career, she accumulated many awards and honors. Known as Lady Magic, she inspired generations of women.

Nancy Lieberman, a standout basketball player at Old Dominion University, led the Lady Monarchs to two consecutive championships. *Courtesy Special Collections & University Archives, Patricia W. & J. Douglas Perry Library, Old Dominion University Libraries.*

August 3

1998—Lucky Streich Hired to Trap Critters at Airport

A Southampton County fellow, Frazier "Lucky" Streich, spent his first day working for officials at Norfolk International Airport, where he was tasked with the responsibility of removing foxes who made their home near the facility. The sly creatures could potentially present safety hazards to the flying public when they darted out onto runways. The thirty-five-year-old professional trapper understood the complexity of his task and the foxes' ability to outwit their adversaries. Of the six traps he initially set, the foxes dismantled three and didn't bother to take the bait.

August 4

1818—Flax Seed Exports Regulated

A series of ordinances was passed this day by the Common Council of the Borough of Norfolk regulating the shipment of flax seed. All flax seed to be shipped from the borough would need to be inspected. It would be unlawful to ship flax seed that was not "well cured, sound and merchantable" and packed in casks of seasoned oak built to the specifications of the ordinance, and all casks were to be marked with initials of the inspector in letters at least three-quarters of an inch. Additionally, all casks of flax seed approved for shipment would be labeled "Norfolk Flax Seed." All of these and other ordinances regulating flax seed would go into effect on September 1, 1818.

August 5

2011—Local Helicopter Squadrons Receive Golden Wrench Award

Sergei Sikorsky, son of aviation pioneer Igor Sikorsky, was in town to present three local groups the prestigious Sikorsky Aircraft Golden Wrench Award that honors superior aircraft maintenance. Helicopter Sea Combat Squadron (HSC) 22's "Sea Knights," HSC 7's "Dusty Dogs" and Helicopter Mine Countermeasures Squadron (HM) 14's "Vanguard" were the distinguished crews that earned the notable accolade that is awarded annually. The presentation took place at Norfolk Naval Station.

Master Chief Petty Officer Douglas Dickinson of the Sea Knights receives the Golden Wrench Award from Sergei Sikorsky. *Photo by Petty Officer Third Class Dustin Good, courtesy of DVIDS.*

August 6

1901—Mile-Wide Tornado Strikes City

On a day filled with unusual weather that included a heavy downpour followed by periods of bright sunshine, an early afternoon tornado hit the Brambleton Ward near downtown. The cyclone came following a hot and still period after a particularly intense rain. Several homes were damaged, and many had their roofs blown off. Chimneys crumbled and windows shattered. A witness to the destruction telephoned the newspaper office, but the report of devastation was thought to be a hoax. Many had never witnessed such a storm, which was described as a mile wide at the top and three feet wide on the ground. No one was injured in the incident.

August 7

1982—Marathoner Spends Birthday in Norfolk

Winner of three back-to-back-to-back New York City Marathons, Alberto Salazar, spent his twenty-fourth birthday in Hampton Roads and met a crowd of runners and admirers at a local sportswear shop. At the time of his visit, he was training for the ten-thousand-meter run and the marathon in the upcoming 1984 Los Angeles Olympic Games. The Cuban native lodged with family during his visit and used his time in the area to train in a climate similar to his upcoming races.

August 8

1900—Hearing Held on Proposed Norfolk and Western Pier

The Board of Harbor Commissioners met this day to consider the construction of a new pier at Lambert's Point by the Norfolk and Western Railroad Company. Two N&W piers were already in operation but were not held in highest esteem by those with business interests in the city. According to written accounts, the current piers were impediments to navigation since they caused the channel through which vessels passed to contract and also created a strong current with the change of tides. No decision was made, and meetings and hearings went on for a week. In the end, a pier to the south of the current N&W piers was permitted with the caveat that if it was ever declared a nuisance to navigation, it would be removed at the expense of the owner.

August 9

1865—Young People's Concert Well Attended

The "smiling and animated" pupils of music instructor J.F. Wilkins gave a concert downtown at the opera house. The children were seated "systematically" and "according to size" and presented a "very beautiful and striking appearance" resembling "young fairies." The children's performances assured that Professor Wilkins was a proper instructor and that he was adept at developing their talent. It was reported that the concert was well attended, especially by the ladies of the city.

August 10

1949—New Rice's Fashion Corner Debuts

Crowds of people turned out despite the Norfolk summer heat to take part in the grand opening of Rice's Fashion Corner at its "uptown" location at the corner of Little Creek Road (then Sewell's Point Road) and Granby Street at Ward's Corner. The event featured a ribbon cutting in front of the sleek escalator. Within three years, a new $350,000 structure that combined both Rice's Fashion Corner and Hofheimer's Shoes again drew crowds for an evening opening from 7:00 to 9:00 p.m. with giveaways such as helium balloons and lambs' wool shoe buffers. The Rice's portion of the building later became LaVogue and Lillian Vernon. The structure was razed in 2000.

White suits, bow ties and boutonnières were fashionable at the ribbon cutting of Rice's Fashion Corner at Ward's Corner. *Courtesy Sargeant Memorial Collection, Norfolk Public Library.*

August 11

2012—Romney Selects Ryan as Running Mate

Republican candidate for U.S. president Mitt Romney announced his running mate, Paul D. Ryan, forty-two-year-old congressman from Wisconsin. Romney made the announcement, which was kept a remarkable secret in the age of Facebook posts and Twitter feeds, at a festive rally of two thousand held aboard the USS *Wisconsin*, a decommissioned battleship berthed downtown. Ryan flew secretively from his home state to Elizabeth City, North Carolina, less than an hour's drive from Norfolk. In his opening remarks, Romney said that the city's "beauty is only matched by its proud heritage as a defender of freedom." The next stop on the campaign trail for Romney and Ryan was North Carolina.

Norfolk made a beautiful backdrop for presidential candidate Mitt Romney to announce Paul Ryan as his running mate. *Photo by James R. Currie.*

August 12

1911—National Clay Court Champions Hail From City

Hugh G. Whitehead and James H. Winston defeated New Orleans's Harvey and Paul McQuiston in five sets. They then put down sitting champions Walter T. Hatch of Chicago and F.G. Anderson of Brooklyn in a challenge match to become the doubles champions at the U.S. clay court championships at the Omaha Field Club in Omaha, Nebraska. According to newspaper reports, "The Virginians entirely outclassed the title holders and there wasn't a moment when the result was in doubt."

August 13

1794—Semi-Weekly Prints First Issue

The *Herald and Norfolk and Portsmouth Advertiser* was first published by Charles Willett. After publishing for over a year, it became a thrice-weekly. During its tenure, the publisher changed to Willett and O'Connor and then later just J. O'Connor. The title changed several times, including the *Herald*, the *Norfolk Herald*, the *Norfolk Advertiser* and *Public Advertiser* and O'Connor's *Norfolk and Portsmouth Herald.*

August 14

1945—City Celebrates War's End

President Harry S. Truman announced that Japan had accepted the terms of the Potsdam Declaration issued on July 26 in which the president told Japan to "surrender or suffer prompt and utter destruction." Impromptu spontaneous celebrations took place across the country and around the globe. In Norfolk, sailors clasped hands with one another and with civilians and performed a snake dance among the cars downtown on Granby Street. It was reported that one person in the city expired from the sheer excitement of the news.

A spontaneous victory celebration on Granby Street. *Photo by Charles Borjes, courtesy Sargeant Memorial Collection, Norfolk Public Library.*

August 15

1953—Colts and Eagles Play Fundraiser Game

The Baltimore Colts and Philadelphia Eagles were in the city to play a night game at Foreman Field. Tickets were $3.60 and proceeds benefited the Joy Fund, an established charity that was in its twentieth year. Because of the segregated nature of the times, the stadium was divided into white and black sections. The Eagles eked out a 10–7 victory before a crowd of thirteen thousand. The game was sponsored by Norfolk Newspapers, Inc. The Joy Fund is still an active charity under the auspices of the *Virginian-Pilot* newspaper.

August 16

1926—Ferries Return to Service

After an all-day meeting, ferry owners reached an agreement to end a strike of twenty or so union navigation pilots and engineers. Regular ferry service resumed between Norfolk and Portsmouth. During the strike, ferry service was limited to two of five vessels on the route, which was just short of a mile. In order to take care of passengers, private vessels made the runs between the port cities. The normal fare for the ferry was five cents, but private carriers could command as much as twenty-five cents.

August 17

1974—Crosby, Stills, Nash and Young Play Foreman Field

One of America's first super groups, the quartet Crosby, Stills, Nash and Young, played a two-and-a-half-hour concert at Old Dominion University's Foreman Field. The afternoon event, attended by an estimated thirty-five thousand, was marked by extreme heat and was part of a tour of open-air stadiums across America organized by promoter Bill Graham. Opening acts were Jessie Collin Young and Elvin Bishop. CSNY opened with Stephen Stills's "Love the One You're With," which opened each concert on what would become known as the Doom Tour. The band played a set of acoustic music followed by a set of electric music. It would be many years before another large-scale concert was held at Foreman Field.

Foreman Field filled to capacity to hear Crosby, Stills, Nash and Young. *Courtesy Special Collections & University Archives, Patricia W. & J. Douglas Perry Library, Old Dominion University Libraries.*

August 18

1879—Storm Hits City, Event Described as Red-Letter Day

Norfolk was in the path of a destructive hurricane that struck the city with record high tides and winds that uprooted trees and blew roofs off dwellings. During the tempest, barometric pressure dropped from 29.58 at 9:00 a.m. to 29.12 a little over two hours later. The event was compared to the storm of June 1825. Winds blew around seventy-five miles per hour in town, and out at Cape Henry, gusts were near one hundred miles per hour. At least six inches of rain fell, and the tide rose, too—seven feet above normal.

August 19

2011—Long-Awaited Light Rail Debuts

The Tide, Hampton Roads Transit's light rail system, carried its first riders on this day. The first 7.4-mile phase had eleven stops, including Norfolk State University, Harbor Park, Norfolk General Hospital and Eastern Virginia Medical School. For the first week, rides were complimentary, and it was estimated that in its first three days, seventy-five thousand people

After much anticipation, the Tide, Norfolk's light rail system, began its route between Eastern Virginia Medical School and Newtown Road. *Photo by James R. Currie.*

took advantage of the special promotion and caught the Tide. Ridership exceeded initial expectations, and a month after the Tide started moving commuters, Norfolk officials suggested an expansion of the system to extend to the naval base.

August 20

1976—Carter and Greene to Campaign for Zumwalt

On this day, colorful Billy Carter, the younger brother of the Democratic nominee for the president of the United States, flew into Norfolk International Airport. He and television star Lorne Greene of *Bonanza* fame hoped to spend the weekend in the city raising money for Elmo Zumwalt Jr. for his bid to capture a Virginia senate seat. Carter believed he would be the brother of the next U.S. president and, when asked about being so close to Suffolk, agreed that it was indeed the Peanut Capital of Virginia, but he believed that Dawson, Georgia—not Suffolk—was the Peanut Capital of the World.

August 21

1896—Sleeping Fisherman Tumbles from Skiff and Drowns

Fisherman Frank Johnson was asleep in a skiff along with Joseph Price, with whom he operated a small fishing business. In order to change position, Johnson moved and hence tumbled out of the drifting boat. The event took place near the Southern Railway docks and was witnessed by an officer walking his beat and the dock's night watchman. Both tried to hail the fisherman but were unable to rouse him. It was reported Johnson sank immediately. P.P. Walker, a mate on the Southern Railway tug *Piedmont* was awakened quickly and then set out in a skiff to look for the missing fisherman. He was unable to find the body. After Price was found still sleeping, he was questioned, jailed for drunkenness and later released.

August 22

1938—Norfolk Teen Rescues Women

Seventeen-year-old Howard Bennington Allard Jr., of the city, pulled in two struggling women from the surf at Chesapeake Beach. Rescued were a local nurse, Miss Lucille Spencer, and her sister, Mrs. Mattie Spencer Ricks, of Conway, North Carolina. Lost in the surf was Ricks's husband of just six weeks, Gilbert Ricks, whose body was later recovered. He went under in six feet of water a short distance from his new wife. It was believed he suffered cramps.

August 23

1933—Hurricane Damages Beaches, Floods Downtown

A fierce hurricane packing winds of eighty miles an hour damaged roofs, blew down trees, flooded city streets and caused electrical outages. At Ocean View, the Nansemond Hotel suffered damage from the high waves. Two of its wings were undermined by the excessive tide. Worst hit was Willoughby Spit, where cottages were washed off foundations, and sand washed in and covered the roads during the storm surge. Firemen, policemen and the

A flooded Granby Street following the hurricane of '33. *Courtesy Sargeant Memorial Collection, Norfolk Public Library.*

Coast Guard rescued many from the perilous ordeal. It was reported that many in that area sought shelter in the ferry terminal. Original estimates of damage were $2 million.

August 24

2009—Court Elevator Back in Service

According to Circuit Clerk George Schaefer, those who needed to attend trials in the six upstairs courtrooms at Norfolk Circuit Court were able to reach them by a newly repaired elevator instead of walking up a flight of stairs. Elevator service had been knocked out because of flooding from heavier-than-normal rainfall. One of the building's elevators had been out of commission for quite some time but had been refurbished with an old motor from an elevator at the old Kirn Memorial Library and was ready to roll when the water damage occurred.

August 25

*1995—*Ledger-Star *Publishes Final Edition*

Nofolk's sole afternoon newspaper, the *Ledger-Star*, published its final issue. The paper began in 1876 as the *Public Ledger*. After a 1906 merger with the *Norfolk Dispatch*, it was known as the *Norfolk Ledger-Dispatch*. It went by its final title after acquiring the *Portsmouth Star* in the 1950s. In its final days, the *Ledger-Star*'s circulation had diminished to only ten thousand subscriptions.

August 26

1970—City to Receive Art Collection

Norfolk mayor Roy B. Martin Jr. and Walter P. Chrysler, son of the Chrysler Corporation's founder, announced that Chrysler's art collection that was currently housed at the Chrysler Museum in Provincetown, Massachusetts, would be moved to Norfolk. The collection contained more than five hundred works of art and was valued at $80 million. Chrysler had a tie to Norfolk after serving in the navy and marrying Jean Ester Outland, a native of the city. The Norfolk Museum of Arts and Sciences and the new concert hall under construction downtown would be named for Walter P. Chrysler.

August 27

1960—Redskins and Eagles Duel at Foreman Field

A crowd of over twenty thousand was on hand to watch a National Football Conference exhibition game between the Washington Redskins and the Philadelphia Eagles. The game was close at the end of the first half after Washington scored a field goal each quarter, and the Eagles scored a touchdown in the second quarter. After a scoreless third quarter, the Eagles soared to victory, riding on a seventeen-point fourth quarter. The final score was 24–6. The match was the first National Football League game played in the city since 1954.

August 28

1963—Busses Leave City for March on Washington

In the predawn hours, a number of busses were loaded with participants who would take part in the March on Washington, officially known by its longer name of March on Washington for Jobs and Economic Freedom. Norfolk attendees, like their southern neighbors in Raleigh and northern neighbors in Baltimore, had the luxury of a fairly short bus ride to the nation's capital. Others from Boston, Little Rock, Milwaukee, Birmingham and St. Louis had much farther to ride. Dr. Martin Luther King Jr. delivered his "I Have a Dream" speech to a quarter million people. The special energy and exuberance of the day was frequently recalled by those fortunate enough to have attended such a monumental event.

August 29

1956—City Awarded Annexation Land

Following a day of riding around the countryside and closed-chamber meetings, a special court of three judges set boundaries for annexation of almost thirteen square miles. Norfolk had filed suit to annex thirty-three miles of Princess Anne County, much of which was already considered urbanized. The increase would bring the city's total area to around fifty-nine square miles. Land added included developed patches along Virginia Beach Boulevard, a populated area between Lake Whitehurst and the municipal airport and East Ocean View. City officials said the land was needed for industrial and residential growth.

August 30

1923—Mob Beats Umpire Harper at Baseball Game

In what was described as an "unprovoked cowardly mob attack," an umpire suffered serious injury. The disgraceful happening was not without far-reaching repercussions. Within two weeks, the president of the National Association of Professional Baseball Clubs set a precedent when he moved to close the Norfolk park where the attack occurred and also fined the owner of the team.

August 31

1971—City Officials Open Beaches for Swimming

Although still restricted from collecting shellfish, Norfolk's Chesapeake Bay beaches were opened for swimming. An eighteen-mile stretch of beaches from Ocean View to Fort Story was closed the day before due to a sewage spill that materialized when Hurricane Doria caused a shutdown of the Chesapeake-Elizabeth sewage treatment facility at Little Creek. Twelve million gallons of chlorine-diluted waste made its way into the Chesapeake Bay. The shellfish closing was projected to last about three weeks. That is about the same amount of time it takes for the bivalves to filter themselves.

SEPTEMBER

September 1

1899—New Routes From City to Europe

The Johnston Steamship Line working with the Southern Railway Company began to make between ten and twelve trips each month from Norfolk to European cities. Hamburg, Antwerp, Rotterdam, London and Liverpool were some of the ports where the steamers *Maplemore* and *Pinemore* would deliver American goods and freight. The increased cargo traffic would mean an additional $3 to $5 million in business for the port.

September 2

1818—Ordinance Calls for Additional Warehouses for Tobacco

The Common Council of the Borough of Norfolk passed an ordinance on this day that appointed a group of commissioners to "take prompt and efficient measures" to improve downtown waterfront properties for the construction of "additional houses for the reception of tobacco" adjacent to one already in existence. The appointed commissioners—John Nivison, George Newton, Thomas Reilly, Thomas Williamson and John Tunis—were authorized to borrow money from banks within the borough in order to get this done.

September 3

1906—Grand Labor Day Celebration Held at Pine Beach

The central labor unions of Norfolk, Portsmouth and Newport News organized an event reported to be "one of the most elaborate ever held in this part of the country." A parade got underway at 10:00 a.m., when labor unions from the sister cities by the sea marched, followed by floats representing their various vocations. The procession, said to be two thousand strong, was led by Norfolk policemen and a number of bands. The marchers ended up at the Norfolk and Atlantic Terminal where special trains took celebrants to Pine Beach to enjoy baseball games, a cake walk and a baby show. Most businesses in the city were closed for the occasion.

September 4

1922—Mayor Roper Opens Norfolk Fair

The Norfolk Fair was formally opened with a short speech by Mayor Albert L. Roper. The six-day event was billed as "The Fair of a Thousand Wonders" and featured agricultural and industrial exhibits, nightly fireworks, auto races, running races and harness races. The fair's organizers hoped to attract visitors and exhibitors from North Carolina and made sure it was known as an interstate fair. Special excursion rates were offered and advertised in towns within one hundred miles, and publicity signs and placards "of the particularly gaudy type" were seen on the many roadways and byways heading into the city.

An advertisement for the Norfolk Fair. *The* Daily Advance *newspaper, Outer Banks History Center Collections.*

September 5

1908—Navy Man in Jail for Sending President Obscene Message

Unable to make bail, naval clerk Arthur Jenkins was sent to the Norfolk Jail for mailing President Teddy Roosevelt what was described as an obscene or scurrilous postcard. Jenkins was awaiting extradition to Connecticut. He was stationed aboard the USS *Scorpion* that was in the Constitution State when he mailed the questionable message. Jenkins was later ordered to the ship *Hancock* in Norfolk for mental observation.

September 6

1948—Brambleton Avenue Business Up in Flames

A three-alarm fire destroyed war surplus valued at $500,000 when Jacob Leitman's Exchange Sales Company burned to the ground. The business, at the corner of East Brambleton Avenue and the Norfolk and Western train tracks, was said to have caught on fire after a train passed around lunchtime. It spread and grew to great intensity when flames reached a cache of cotton mattresses.

September 7

1835—Hero of Fort Fisher Born

William Lamb, who would serve as mayor of Norfolk, as did his father and grandfather before him, was born. He attended the Norfolk Academy, Rappahannock Academy and Military Institute and the College of William and Mary, where he earned a law degree in 1855. Being too young to practice, Lamb got involved with a Norfolk newspaper, the *Southern Argus*, as a partial owner and editor. During the Civil War, Lamb served as commandant of Fort Fisher for two and a half years. The fort was the largest earthwork fortification in the Confederacy and defended the entrance to Wilmington, North Carolina, the last major Southern port that remained open during the war. Following the "late unpleasantness," Colonel Lamb returned to Norfolk and capitalized on the relationships he made with former blockade runners. He worked toward bolstering the city's commerce by taking advantage of steamship lines and railroads.

September 8

1955—Judge Hands Out Sentence for Nudist Magazines

Claiming that "in the State of Virginia we live in a clothed civilization," police justice Savory Amoto contended that the nudist magazine *Sunshine and Health* was obscene and levied suspended fines against three Norfolk men who owned or were employed at area newsstands where the magazine was sold. The fines were suspended because two of the defendants believed it was legal to sell the magazine. The periodicals were confiscated in a raid the month before, and publishers were considering an appeal.

September 9

1879—West Coast Paper Reports on Norfolk Oysters

The *Los Angeles Herald* ran a short article on its front page, above the crease, relaying information shared by the president of the Oyster Packing Association of Norfolk. According to the article, the oyster industry in Virginia had grown significantly following the Civil War, with three million bushels harvested each year. One-third of the shellfish harvest was handled by packers in Norfolk and Portsmouth. At $0.35 a bushel, this made for a $350,000 industry for the cities. The popular delicacies were shipped to port cities far and wide.

September 10

2013—Something to Cluck About: City Council Okays Yard Birds

Norfolk City Council voted six to two to allow residents who lived on lots ten thousand square feet or larger to raise backyard chickens. The ordinance allowed for up to four hens. Councilman Tommy Smigiel suggested lowering the square footage to five thousand square feet. Councilwoman Angela Williams wanted to grandfather in any chicken keepers already raising birds who did not meet the ten-thousand-square-foot code. Councilwoman Theresa Whibley questioned how it was determined that ten thousand square foot would be an appropriate limit. While the pro-chicken law was passed, according an article in the *Virginian-Pilot* two months later, its stringent rules dissuaded yard bird expansion within the city.

September 11

1940—Refugee Ship SS Quanza *Held Over in Norfolk*

The Portuguese passenger ship *Quanza* was ported in Norfolk after stopping for coal. The vessel's odyssey began when it left Lisbon on August 8 with over three hundred passengers, most of whom were trying to flee Europe. The ship landed in New York eleven days later, where close to two hundred passengers disembarked, about one-third of those American citizens. The

The SS *Quanza,* which carried many European Jewish refugees seeking asylum, stopped at Norfolk in 1940. *Photo by Charles Borjes, courtesy Sargeant Memorial Collection, Norfolk Public Library.*

Quanza then traveled to Veracruz, Mexico, where thirty-five passengers were allowed to leave. Eighty-six passengers, mostly Belgian Jews, were on the ship when it arrived at Norfolk. While in port, a Jewish maritime lawyer, Jacob Morewitz, filed a suit for a handful of passengers. Jewish leaders rallied. Eleanor Roosevelt enlisted the help of her husband, the president, who sent an official to investigate. All eighty-six passengers were declared political refugees. Eighty left the ship and entered America. Six voluntarily went back to Europe.

September 12

1855—Yellow Fever Grips City

Forty-five people died from yellow fever on this day, and fifty new cases were diagnosed. The viral disease thrived in tropical and semitropical climates and was spread by infected mosquitos. In the month of August, 560 deaths had been reported. Newspaper accounts described a scene of melancholy suffering. Among the dead were a number of doctors. Donations were raised in many cities, including New Orleans, Baltimore, Philadelphia and Albany. Of special concern were the children left orphaned by the horrible disease. The people of Portsmouth, across the Elizabeth River, also suffered greatly in the epidemic. Nearby Suffolk did not report any cases, but its citizens waited apprehensively.

September 13

1896—Bank Street Church Welcomes New Pastor

On this day at 11:30 a.m., the Bank Street Baptist Church, a black congregation within the city, held a special service welcoming and recognizing its new pastor, H.H. Mitchell, DD, of Farmville, Virginia, proclaimed by the *Richmond Planet* newspaper as "one of the ablest divines of the Baptists of the State." An appropriate sendoff and farewell was held in Farmvillle the following month at the home of Mr. and Mrs. H.P. Bland, which was described as "beautifully lighted." After enjoying the "delicacies of the season," the guests shared their sentiments with Dr. and Mrs. Mitchell and departed.

September 14

1911—League of Municipalities Delegates Head to Cape Charles

About sixty members of the League of Virginia Municipalities left Norfolk aboard the steamer *Pennsylvania* bound for Cape Charles. T.H. Wallace, of the Norfolk Board of Aldermen, addressed the group after the mayor of Cape Charles's welcome. Additional Norfolk influences at the meeting included an address by Mayor Riddick, a presentation on "germ-carrying insects and methods of their destruction" by Norfolk health commissioner Powhatan S. Schenck and a solo sung by Professor Edward W. von Berggrun, which was reported as being "heartily encored."

September 15

1946—Unruly Fans Attack Three Umpires

Following a playoff baseball game between the Norfolk Tars and Roanoke Red Sox, three Piedmont League umpires were caught in a terrible and wild scene. While heading off the field following the final out in the game, a crowd reported to be as large as forty people expressed their dissatisfaction with a call made during the seventh inning. The umpires were taken to Norfolk General Hospital and were treated for lacerations, bruises, lost teeth and a broken nose. Norfolk won the game, 4–2.

September 16

1924—Maryland Sailor Confesses to Robbery

Detectives questioned and later arrested John Y. Offutt, a sailor from Baltimore stationed in Norfolk. The nineteen-year-old drew attention to himself when he appeared in local jewelry stores with a pair of opera glasses and a ring of significant worth. When under interrogation, Offutt's testimony contained inconsistencies, which detectives questioned. After becoming defiant, the boy, said to come from a good Maryland family, confessed. The stolen loot was taken from the home of Captain S.B. Brooks of Towson, Maryland. Offutt and an accomplice skimmed the best from two trunks of contraband and left the remainder in a forested area near the Brookses' home.

September 17

1943—Twenty-Four Killed in Deadly Blast at Base

A massive catastrophic explosion occurred at the Norfolk Naval Base after a three-hundred-pound depth charge exploded and detonated twenty-three others. The blast was heard throughout Hampton Roads and sent an inferno five hundred feet in the air. The bombs were filled with a new deadly mix of chemicals, Torpex, that was later replaced because of its instability. In addition to those who died in the explosion, an estimated 250 were wounded. Among those killed was Elizabeth Korensky, who was serving as a Woman Accepted for Voluntary Emergency Service (WAVES). Korensky was the only woman in that branch of the military to die in service during World War II.

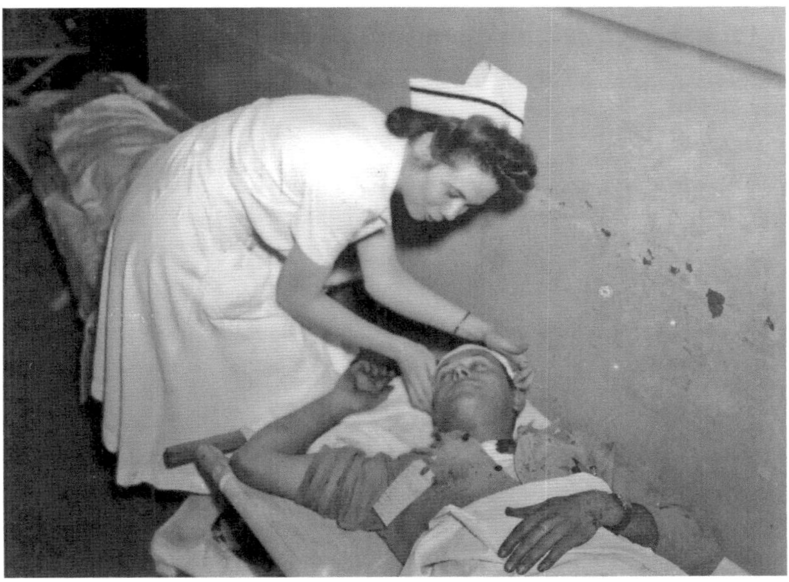

A nurse at St. Vincent's Hospital tends to a man wounded in the explosion at the Norfolk Naval Base. *Photo by Charles Borjes, courtesy Sargeant Memorial Collection, Norfolk Public Library.*

September 18

2003—Hurricane Isabel Leaves Watery Calling Card

Just after the peak of hurricane season, Hurricane Isabel's storm surge, which was between seven and eight feet, brought unprecedented flooding to the city, even rivaling the Hurricane of August 1933. Downtown and Ghent were inundated with rising water that flooded the Midtown Tunnel, while at Ocean View the Chesapeake Bay's pounding waves damaged waterfront homes and destroyed Harrison's Fishing Pier. With wind gusts of eighty miles per hour, Isabel also downed many trees throughout the city. The storm made landfall in North Carolina as a Category 2 storm and was a Category 1 storm when it reached Norfolk.

September 19

2010—Jamz103 Program Director Passes

Lawrence Brown III, known professionally as Kool DJ Law, was called home this day. The Frederick, Maryland native was forty years old. Brown was well known as a DJ on JAMZ103, where he had worked for nearly twenty years. He and Christopher "Big B" Belcher paired and made up the popular Boodah Brothers, who enjoyed a long career on JAMZ103. Many rap artists credited Brown with helping their records break. While Brown and Belcher could've moved to larger radio markets, their love of the region kept them in Hampton Roads. Brown is said to have popularized the term "The Seven Cities" to refer to the listening area he served, which was made up of Norfolk, Virginia Beach, Chesapeake, Suffolk, Portsmouth, Hampton and Newport News.

September 20

1857—Survivors From Wreck of Central America *Recuperate*

Approximately twenty women along with a number of children who lived through the sinking of the steamship *Central America* were recuperating in the city, having been brought to Norfolk. The ship ran into a hurricane, sprang a leak and sank two hundred miles off Cape Hatteras on September

12, taking with it mail from California and over $1.5 million in gold. Four hundred passengers and crew members drowned. The survivors were housed at the National Hotel, where local ladies came to their aid. A call went out through the town, and soon a large collection of women's and children's clothing had been gathered, along with cash donations. The shipwrecked ladies sincerely expressed their "gratitude for the kindness with which we were treated by the people of Norfolk."

September 21

1972—Sandwich Company to Expand

Norfolk-based Stewart Sandwiches, Inc., received a $1.75 million expansion opportunity in order to double the size of the company's production facility. The company, which made famous cold premade sandwiches that were heated in special ovens and sold at convenience markets and truck stops, got its start in 1958 by Van H. Cunningham and T.J. Broeker. The expansion deal was arranged by the Norfolk Port and Industrial Authority and would allow the company to manufacture its own hamburger patties instead of purchasing them. Burgers made up 45 percent of the company's sandwich sales. Five hundred people were employed around the country by the sandwich firm, which grossed $1.3 million annually.

September 22

1914—Virginia Votes Dry, Norfolk and Other Cities Vote No

On this day, Virginia citizens voted to enact prohibition, making it illegal to sell spirited drinks. The drys outnumbered the wets by forty thousand, and the law was set to go into effect on November 1, 1916. This was three years before national prohibition was enacted in 1919, and the issue was much covered by the local press. Four cities voted against the statewide prohibition, including Norfolk. The other wet cities were Alexandria, close to our nation's capital; Richmond, the state capital; and Williamsburg, first state capital and home of the College of William and Mary.

September 23

1980—City to Ration Water

After a particularly hot and dry summer that left area reservoirs just above half-capacity, Norfolk City Council made the decision to begin water rationing at the end of the month. City Manager Julian F. Hirst shared the news that consumers would be asked to consume only 75 percent of their average use. The navy and the cities of Virginia Beach and Chesapeake all received water from Norfolk. The voluntary restrictions went into effect on October 1. Everyone hoped for rain.

September 24

2005—Irish Wake Held For Norfolk Rebel *Captain*

Friends and family came out to celebrate the life of Captain Lane Briggs, who did much to promote the rich maritime history and heritage of Norfolk. He crossed the horizon on September 19 at the age of seventy-three. The Tar Heel native spent the first fifteen years of his life near Mars Hill, before making his way to the coast. His love of the water kept him near it for the remainder of his life. Lane was the founder of the Great Chesapeake Bay Schooner Race and was influential in the creation of Norfolk's maritime celebration, Harborfest. The innovative Briggs also created the *Norfolk Rebel*, which he dubbed a tugantine. It was a traditional tug, rigged with sails to operate under wind power. His Rebel Marine Service was based at Willoughby. It was said of Captain Briggs that if you weren't his friend, he hadn't met you yet.

September 25

1907—Despondent Father Kills Self

After learning that his family would be evicted from their home, an unemployed trolley operator took his own life. The man, who was seeking to learn his family's whereabouts, went to the home of his brother in the Lambert's Point section of the city. When unable to determine where his wife and children were, he asked his brother to come outside to see a trick. It was at that point that the pitiful fellow put the gun to his temple and ended his life.

September 26

1949—Military Brass See Carrier First Hand

As the final portion of the Joint Civilian Orientation Conference organized by the National Military Establishment, an assemblage of vessels departed Norfolk led by Louis Johnson, United States secretary of defense. Along for the expedition was a distinguished group that included Secretary of the Air Force Stuart Symington and General Omar Bradley aboard the carrier *Franklin D. Roosevelt*. They witnessed a day's worth of operations at sea, including the bomber *Neptune* taking off from the aircraft carrier *Midway*. Also along for the expedition were eighty civilians who represented various national interests. The purpose of the trip was to allow for an up-close view of what U.S. Navy sea power and aviation could achieve.

September 27

1903—Priest Admonishes Congregation

John J. Doherty, rector of St. Mary's Roman Catholic Church, spoke out during Sunday mass and scolded his congregants for spitting in the sanctuary. The assertive Doherty said that spitting in church was defiling the house of God. He claimed to have a good idea of who the culprits were but said he would employ the use of informants to ensure the "expectorators" would be caught. The good Father intended to read the list of perpetrators at mass and have them arrested for violating the city ordinance against spitting in public buildings.

September 28

1865—Chief of Freedman's Bureau Visits City

General Oliver Otis Howard visited Norfolk on his tour through the South. Howard had the challenging task of helping former slaves who had gained their freedom during the Civil War assimilate into mainstream society. This was not easily accomplished, as the freedmen had little or no capital or property. During his visit, Howard met with Mayor Tabb of Norfolk, Mayor Collins of Portsmouth and other city officials. Howard, whose address was described as "conciliatory, calm and dignified," called for the "hearty cooperation of

General Oliver Otis Howard, head of the Freedman's Bureau, visited Norfolk in 1865. *Brady-Handy Collection, Library of Congress.*

the people in carrying out the wishes of the President to assist in the establishment of his humane policy in regard to the administration of justice, among the freedmen." The general was more or less pleased with the state of things in Virginia and hoped that the Norfolk area would be "found in a like progressive position."

September 29

2011—Officials Urge Citizens to Steer Clear of Elizabeth River

Water samples were collected and tested following a sewage leak the night before. Officials from the Hampton Roads Sanitation District warned of coming in contact with water from the Elizabeth River. The sewage spill, estimated at over 600,000 gallons, occurred following a power outage at a treatment plant on Powhatan Avenue near Old Dominion University. With the onslaught of approaching storms, authorities switched to generator power at the plant, but the generator did not operate as needed. Activities that caused direct contact with river water and were to be avoided included swimming, paddling, boating and fishing. The area of concern stretched from Lambert's Point to the Lafayette River.

September 30

1915—Captain of Greek Steamer Charged with Stowaways

P.D. Hanos, captain of the ship *Dionyssios Stathatos*, appeared before U.S. Commissioner Percy Stephenson, who charged the Greek captain to appear before the next grand jury in Norfolk Federal Court. Hanos was accused of taking on four stowaways in Barcelona, Spain, who were not allowed to disembark in Oran, Algeria. The Greek ship continued on to Norfolk, where Hanos failed to report the extra passengers. When two left the ship, Inspector Morton, of the Norfolk Immigration Bureau, had a warrant issued for the captain.

OCTOBER

October 1

1950—Ocean View Netters Haul Record Catch

One of the largest catches in recent memory was made when two seine netters, Mr. J.C. Williams and Mr. J.W. Haywood, set their nets in a channel near the Cape Charles ferry terminal. Their nets collected sixty thousand pounds of fish, made up of puppy drum, croaker and speckled trout. Photographer Jim Mays captured several images of local residents coming forward and assisting in the haul. The fish netted Williams and Haywood $15,000.

The big haul at Ocean View. *Photo by Jim Mays, courtesy Sargeant Memorial Collection, Norfolk Public Library.*

October 2

1921—Peanut Growers Move Office From Suffolk to Norfolk

The Peanut Growers Exchange moved its headquarters to Norfolk and set up shop in the Southern Commercial Produce building, on the fifth floor. The office space would be remodeled and updated to suit the needs of its new occupants. All business would be conducted from the new and more centrally located office, and a membership drive in southeastern Virginia and northeastern North Carolina was planned. Collective marketing of area peanuts was a goal of the Peanut Growers Exchange.

October 3

1977—Woman Receives Sentence and Bus Fare

Judge William L. Shapero gave a woman a thirty-day suspended sentence after she was charged with disorderly conduct. The perpetrator, described as middle aged, had sought shelter at the city jail when her public assistance check was late. It was there that she became unruly and was arrested. In addition to her suspended sentence, the judge gave the woman fifty cents in order to catch the bus to Titustown to save her the walk.

October 4

2012—Eagle Nest Removed from Garden

After nearly ten years at Norfolk Botanical Garden, an active eagle nest was removed because the large birds of prey were considered dangerous to air traffic in and out of nearby Norfolk International Airport. Four of the raptors had been killed by airplanes during that time period. The eagles were very popular and were observed and enjoyed by many after an "eagle cam" was installed prior to the 2006 nesting season. The decision to remove the nest was made after a twelve-month study in which eagles were often seen feeding and resting on the airport's runways.

October 5

1896—Fair Opens and Is Deemed Success, Crowds Expected All Week

An agricultural and mechanical fair opened and was deemed a success on this day. The fine autumn weather no doubt helped to bring out the crowds. It was the first fair of this type held in Norfolk in several years. The event was organized by the Norfolk Driving Club and Fair Association and featured exhibits, described as "exceedingly credible," placed on display by merchants from both Norfolk and Portsmouth. Typical attractions included were candy vendors, photography booths, shooting galleries and pink lemonade. Horse races were another mentionable draw with "many fine horses" from a number of midatlantic states engaged in the matches. A Richmond horse won the "big stake."

October 6

1916—Fog Causes Collision

The Chesapeake Steamship Company's *City of Norfolk* was leaving port for Baltimore with approximately one hundred passengers when it struck the British tramp steamer *Hawkhead* anchored near Sewell's Point. Those aboard the *City of Norfolk* were moved onto the steamer *Pocahontas* and then onto another steam vessel to continue their journey. The *Hawkhead* sank within fifteen minutes, and those aboard were picked up by the "small boats" from the *Norfolk* and *Pocahontas* and other vessels in the harbor at the time of the accident. The mishap occurred around 8:00 p.m. in heavy fog.

October 7

1918—Spanish Influenza Grips City

Norfolk and Portsmouth were suffering with thousands of new cases of influenza and more than three dozen deaths within a day's time. Ordinances were passed closing pool halls and barbershops in an attempt to curb the spread of the epidemic. Restaurants were ordered to sterilize all cutlery, service pieces and utensils. Cold weather and a fierce wind were thought to exacerbate the conditions for coming down with the disease, and soldiers and sailors on furlough added to the carriers and potential victims of the virus. State officials would eventually cancel the upcoming state fair. A week later, it was estimated that there were 200,000 cases in Virginia.

October 8

1909—Plans for Tunnel Revealed

A wire story was released on this day with news that a petition would be presented at the November meeting of the Norfolk City Council to obtain permits to construct a railroad tunnel under the Elizabeth River. The plan was to connect lines of the Atlantic Coast Line, Seaboard Air Line and Southern Railway to enter the city and would connect with rail lines of the Norfolk Southern Line to Cape Henry. It was believed that it would be more economically viable to build a breakwater and piers at Cape Henry for transatlantic trade than to have steamers come into Norfolk. Also proposed was a $1 million downtown union railway depot.

October 9

1861—Prisoners Captured on Union Gunboat Fanny *Brought to City*

Over sixty soldiers, sailors, cooks and crewmen were brought to the city after they were captured on the Union vessel *Fanny* during an engagement known as the Chicamacomico Races on North Carolina's Hatteras Island. A local paper said that while the prisoners attracted much attention, they were not mistreated and were in good spirits. Norfolk was under Confederate control, and Colonel Benjamin Huger (pronounced OO-jhey) was in charge of operations in the city. Although under martial law, it was said that Northern interests were more tolerated in Norfolk than other parts of the state, as long as no one expressed "sentiments antagonistic to the Southern cause."

October 10

*1954—*Mormackite *Survivors Land at Norfolk*

Eleven survivors from the Greek freighter *Mormackite* arrived in the city after a harrowing ordeal. The vessel was en route from Buenos Aires to Baltimore three days earlier when high seas caused a shift of its cargo, which made the *Mormackite* list and consequently sink. Of the freighter's crew of forty-eight, eleven were rescued and twelve bodies were recovered. After the men landed in the water, a handful died after being bitten by sharks. The spouse of one of the *Mormackite*'s crew was waiting for her husband in Baltimore when she received word of the vessel's fate. She rushed to Norfolk and met the survivors. Mrs. Wall pleaded for information about her husband, but he was not among those who made it.

October 11

1983—City Surveyor Rescues Woman

Thirty-year-old Bobbie J. Person drove her car off Bell's Bridge and, being unable to swim, she began to call (by voice, not on a cellphone) for help. Edward Baldwin, a surveyor with the city, heard Mrs. Person's cries and removed his jacket and dove into the Lafayette River to rescue the driver from her slowly sinking vehicle. A construction worker on a job nearby also entered the water and aided the pair. No one was injured in the incident.

October 12

1899—Spitters to Be Fined

On this day, a law went into effect that banned spitting in public places such as on sidewalks, in elevators and on streetcars. In order to publicize the new legislation, placards were made up under the direction of the Board of Health and were placed in various public spots in the city. A fine between one and five dollars would be levied on those who violated the law. Shortly after the ordinance was passed, it was reported that folks were seen spitting in the gutter or the street. Roanoke, Virginia, followed suit the following month and passed its own anti-spiting ordinance.

October 13

2006—Former Mayor, City Leader and Retired Obstetrician Passes

Mason Andrews, who was estimated to have delivered five thousand babies and was instrumental in the creation of the Eastern Virginia Medical School, died in Norfolk on this day. Andrews, a Norfolk native, served on the city council for twenty-six years and was mayor between 1992 and 1994. Dr. Andrews played a key role in the redevelopment of the city's downtown, especially the waterfront. Nauticus, Town Point Park, Waterside and MacArthur Center were all revitalization projects to which he lent his efforts. Andrews was also known for delivering the country's first "test tube baby" in 1981.

October 14

1894—Teen Begins Sixty-Year Newspaper Career

A month shy of his fourteenth birthday, E.M. Holmes began working at the *Norfolk Pilot* newspaper as a copy boy. In a few short years, he was made city editor of the *Norfolk Landmark*, and in 1912, he made a switch over to the *Ledger Dispatch*. During his sixty-year career, Holmes covered major events for the newspapers and served in roles as various as a crime and court reporter to theater and movie critic. The city native retired in 1956 and died on Christmas Eve day at the age of eighty-two.

October 15

1852—Centegenarian Billy Passes, Witness To History

A man of color named Billy, 117 years old, died in Norfolk on this day. He was born in Hanover County, Virginia, and was said to be in Norfolk during the British invasion of the city in 1776 and remembered the Battles at Great Bridge and Yorktown. In his later years, he was a drayman (one who drove a cart pulled by a horse, mule or ox). Billy was described as strong, hale and hearty, good-natured and honest. When Billy died, he was the property of the late Mrs. Sarah Ingram.

October 16

2004—Renovated Attucks Theater Reopens

What was known during its heyday as "the Apollo Theater of the South," the Attucks Theater at Church Street and Virginia Beach Boulevard, began a new chapter in its history after an $8 million renovation. Built in 1919, the Attucks was designed, backed and operated by black talent and capital, and it served as a premiere venue for Norfolk's black community segregated from white society according to the mores of the times. Duke Ellington, B.B. King and local songstress Ruth Brown from Portsmouth-town delighted audiences at the 625-seat Attucks, which was later known as the Booker T. The Preservation Hall Jazz Band played for the grand reopening.

October 17

1899—Oyster Shuckers Begin Strike

A decision in the city not to employ union workers led to a strike of oyster shuckers, who played an important role in getting the shellfish delicacy to market. On strike were 500 shuckers, a vocation dominated by black Norfolkians, with an additional 1,200 expected in the coming days. It was estimated that the oyster trade in the city was worth $2 million, the upcoming strike would cripple the industry and as many as five thousand workers would be affected by the strike.

October 18

1940—Defense Housing Project Begun

In order to meet the growing need to house military and defense construction workers and their families, groundbreaking took place for Merrimack Park, a five-hundred-unit housing project for married enlisted personnel. The residents moved in in April the following year. Single-story freestanding homes, duplexes and two-story multi-family dwellings and apartments were included in the complex. Merrimack Park was built by the United States Housing Authority at a cost of just under $2 million. The project was dedicated in October 1941 with much pomp and festivity.

Groundbreaking at Merrimac Park, a five-hundred-unit development built to house defense workers. *Photo by Charles Borjes, courtesy Sargeant Memorial Collection, Norfolk Public Library.*

October 19

1936—Retired Assistant Surgeon General Dies on Steamer Near City

Pasquotank County, North Carolina native Dr. James Clifford Perry died aboard the steamer *District of Columbia* near Norfolk. Dr. Perry resided in San Francisco but had come east to visit family and to present an impressive collection of Chinese porcelain to the Norfolk Museum of Arts and Sciences in memory of his departed wife. In addition to serving as the assistant surgeon general, Perry also served as medical director of the U.S. Public Health Service and worked at Ellis Island and in the Panama Canal Zone. He is buried at Elmwood Cemetery in Norfolk.

October 20

1905—Heatherbloom Sets High Jump Record

On the final day of the second-annual Norfolk Horse Show, the horse Heatherbloom jumped a barrier of seven feet ten inches, breaking his own record by one inch. The four-day event was held in the Norfolk Coliseum, which was decorated in orange, blue and white, the colors of the Norfolk Horse Show Association. The show drew entries from five states that competed for their share of prize money. Governor Montague of Virginia and Governor Dawson of West Virginia were honored guests, as were several high-ranking naval officers. Special transportation within the city and from points on the peninsula and eastern North Carolina was arranged.

October 21

1865—Man Misses Gangway, Lands in Harbor

While the steamer *Dictator* was leaving its wharf for a voyage to Richmond, a man ran to the vessel and tried to make his way aboard. While jumping for the ship, he missed the gangway and ended up in the water. The ship's clerk, Captain D.H. Hill, responded to the call of "man over board" and successfully pulled the man up to safety. It was at this point that the rescued man, who was described as "dripping like an otter," offered Captain Hill these words, "You're a damn fool. I've got no money."

October 22

1824—City Fêtes Marquis de Lafayette

French aristocrat and ally in the American Revolution, Gilbert du Motier, Marquis de Lafayette spent a number of days in Norfolk on his visit to America. He arrived on the steamer *Petersburg* and was welcomed by the mayor, John E. Holt. Lafayette was greeted by the citizens of the city, his way adorned by flower petals strewn by the borough's children. During his stay, receptions, banquets and balls described as lavish were held to mark Lafayette's visit. The *Norfolk Herald* reported that both Norfolk and Portsmouth were decorated with displays of lights at night.

October 23

1968—Give Back the Money, Says Secret Service

The Secret Service instructed the public to hand over any counterfeit money received that had been printed to announce the presidential candidacy of Peace and Freedom Party nominee, comedian and social activist Dick Gregory. The groundbreaking Gregory and his aides were in Norfolk the week before handing out the dollars that were similar to regular U.S. dollar bills but instead had Gregory's picture where George Washington should have been. The Secret Service said that reproducing United States currency in such form violated several laws and so it had to be confiscated.

October 24

1978—Norfolk State College Looks to Rise to University

College president Harrison B. Wilson let it be known that Norfolk State College would petition the Virginia General Assembly to gain university status. Founded in 1935 as an affiliate of Richmond's Virginia Union University, Norfolk State was one of Virginia's traditionally black colleges. Coincidentally, Virginia State College in Richmond—another historically black college with which Norfolk State was affiliated for twenty-five years—had recently put in such a request. In 1969, Norfolk's Old Dominion College, which began in 1930 as a satellite of the College of William and Mary, gained university status.

October 25

1899—Concert Raises Funds for St. Vincent's

An ample crowd gathered at the Academy of Music for a concert given under the auspices of the Norfolk Council 367 of the Knights of Columbus in order to raise money for the building fund of St. Vincent's Hospital. The audience was reported to be enthusiastic and generous with its praise, which would account for the number of callbacks and encores during the presentation. The event transpired under the guidance of James W. Casey, Professor A.L. Koerner and W.H. Jones. Miss L. de Russey Berry was the accompanist for the evening.

October 26

1895—Guests Tour New Steamship Pinners Point

Forty or so influential railroad and businessmen were invited guests of Captain David Jenkins to inspect the new freight steamer *Pinners Point* of the North American Transport Company. It had recently arrived from England on its first run of a new weekly service between Norfolk and Liverpool. The ship was docked at Lamberts Point receiving a load of cotton. The guests arrived by tug, and after an hour of touring and viewing the fine appointments on the ship, the group moved to the saloon, where seasonal delicacies such as turkey and lobster were served. Cut-glass dishes laden with bon-bons were placed at choice places on the table. Well-trained waiters attended to the guests, but the gathering was described as informal, and "everybody was made to feel at home."

October 27

1980—Navy Okays Norfolk to Tap Into Suffolk Water

On this day, navy officials granted Norfolk permission to dig wells on federal property in Suffolk. A hot, dry summer had prompted Norfolk to initiate water cutbacks and rationing, which would have caused a hardship on the navy, so a solution was sought that would help the navy and its homeport city. Suffolk officials were caught off guard by the decision. By the time a Norfolk city truck arrived at the site of the proposed wells the next day, it was met by thirty-five protesters from the Peanut City who lived near the federal lands.

October 28

1939—Navy Day Celebrated in Style

Navy Day, established by the Navy League of the United States and first celebrated in 1922, was in its seventeenth year and was commemorated at the Norfolk Naval Base with flyovers and a dress parade inspected by Rear Admiral Joseph K. Taussig and congressional representative Colgate W. Darden Jr. Ten thousand people were also on hand to view the dress parade

Airplanes fly in formation as part of the Navy Day celebration. *Photo by Charles Borjes, courtesy Sargeant Memorial Collection, Norfolk Public Library.*

and to hear Admiral Taussig address the assembled crowd. October 27, or a date nearby, was selected to celebrate Navy Day, as it was the birthday of Theodore Roosevelt, a supporter of the navy.

October 29

1947—Fanfare Accompanies Debut of "Times Square of the South"

Crowds gathered and bands played to mark the opening of Wards Corner, a shopping plaza at the intersection of Granby Street and Little Creek Road. The commercial center had a modest start when a downtown merchant, Alfred C. Ward, opened a gas station and general store at the corner of Granby Street and Sewells Point Road (later Little Creek Road). In the 1920s, the Teggs opened up a log cabin restaurant featuring barbecue sandwiches opposite Ward's store. Following World War II, the area accelerated into a one-of-a-kind "uptown" shopping center. Growing up in Norfolk, one frequently heard, "Well, I remember Wards Corner when it was just a cornfield."

A crowd assembled and a brass band played to mark the opening of Ward's Corner. *Courtesy Sargeant Memorial Collection, Norfolk Public Library.*

October 30

2012—Fraim Wants Federal Funds To Fix Flooding

The day after Hurricane Sandy devastated the Jersey Shore and caused typical neighborhood flooding in Norfolk's low-lying areas, city officials met with state legislators to draw attention to the city's watery plight. Norfolk was at risk of having portions of the city cut off if storm conditions caused catastrophic flooding, as seen in New Jersey and New York City. Mayor Paul Fraim hoped to keep politicians aware of Norfolk's vulnerability and to gain federal funds for major flood mitigation projects. "What happened just north of here could have easily happened to us," warned Fraim.

October 31

1932—Explosion in Confectionary Kills Man

James Campas, known locally as the "Watermelon King," was found dead, and others were injured following a suspicious explosion at Gretes' confectionary store. The blast, which set the building aflame, destroyed the interior of the business and shattered windows, littering Brambleton Avenue. Following an immediate investigation, police arrested Nick Gretes, the shop's owner, the following day.

NOVEMBER

November 1

1957—Bridge Tunnel Connects Norfolk and Hampton

The Hampton Roads Bridge Tunnel, the three-and-a-half-mile span that connects Norfolk's Willoughby Spit and Hampton's Phoebus section, opened and replaced a ferry route. The project was funded by highway bonds, which were repaid with tolls collected on the Hampton side of the tunnel for many years. The day was marred by a fierce nor'easter that forced ceremonies indoors. It was predicted that by joining the south side and the peninsula, it would merge into a metropolis of over half a million people.

November 2

1906—Norfolk Firms Receive Charters for Jamestown Exposition

Colonial Virginia, Inc., was awarded a charter by the Virginia State Corporation Commission. The Norfolk outfit would create scenes of colonial days in Virginia for display at the upcoming Jamestown Exposition to be held near Willoughby in 1907. Two additional Norfolk firms were granted charters this day as well—the Monarch Laundry Company and the Exposition Hotel Corporation.

November 3

1887—Life of Military Leader Honored

Funeral services were held for Major William H. Palmer, leader of the second battalion of the Virginia Colored Volunteers. Palmer began his military career at the end of the Civil War and during its aftermath, when he served in the Thirty-sixth Regiment of the U.S. Colored Troops. He mustered out as a quartermaster sergeant. The funeral service was held at the Bute Street Baptist Church. It was said to be the largest funeral for a person of color in the city up until that time.

November 4

2012—USS Enterprise Makes Final Trip to Port

On a breezy, seasonal autumn day, the first nuclear-powered aircraft carrier, USS *Enterprise*, returned from its twenty-fifth deployment during its fifty-one-year history. Over ten thousand navy families and people connected with the *Enterprise* were on hand for the special occasion to welcome home

Family and friends wait to welcome the USS *Enterprise* home after its final deployment. *Photo by Petty Officer 2nd Class Rafael Martie, courtesy of DVIDS.*

over five thousand officers and sailors. During its time, the *Enterprise* aided in the 1961 Cuban Missile Crisis and served during Operation Enduring Freedom and Operation New Dawn. The "Big E" was officially deactivated on December 1 and then the following summer moved over to Newport News—a step in the dismantling process.

November 5

1906—Famished Crew Seeks Provisions

The three-masted schooner *Elizabeth Gilbert* made a stop in Norfolk to take on supplies. The 482-ton vessel was reported as halfway between Cape Henry, Virginia, and Barnegat, New Jersey, when the crew decided to make for port. All aboard for sustenance was a small bit of oatmeal with no water for cooking or even to drink. *Elizabeth Gilbert* sailed from Mayport, Florida, for New York on October 19, laden with lumber. The following day, it sailed into a hurricane and took on water. After a broken pump was repaired, the ship ran into a fierce gale. Out of victuals and battling fierce headwinds in a storm that tousled ships along the northeast coast, the *Elizabeth Gilbert* headed for Norfolk.

November 6

1928—Voter Turnout Heavy After Lively Campaign

Precinct balloting sites were reported as congested, and citizens found it necessary to stand in line for hours to cast their votes. The pleasant and seasonal weather drew the populace out for what was predicted to be the largest showing at the polls in state history. In addition to several statewide races, at stake was the presidency of the United States. Norfolk, along with the rest of the state, chose Republican Herbert Hoover over Democrat Al Smith. Locally, Menalcus Lankford defeated incumbent Joseph T. Deal, both of Norfolk, for a seat in the seventy-first Congress.

November 7

2000—Norfolk Voters Want Directly Elected Mayor

City voters on this day cast their ballots in favor of the direct election of the mayor instead of keeping the status quo with city council members choosing the city's leader. Turnout was heavy in the advisory referendum balloting. Norfolk's ward system had been altered in 1992 following the 1990 census and had four white wards and three black wards. Mayor Paul Fraim commented that he was "extremely pleased with the results." He was in favor of moving forward asking the U.S. Justice Department and the General Assembly to approve a change in the city's charter.

November 8

1854—Group Meets to Chart Improvements

Norfolk welcomed the Internal Improvements Convention of Virginia to the city. The assembly was held at the Cumberland Street Baptist Church. During the two-day meeting, several speeches were given and resolutions passed. Issues of importance raised at the convention were the benefit of initiating steamer traffic between Norfolk and European port cities, improving internal navigation through the use of railroads and also connecting the Ohio River and the Chesapeake Bay. The latter was mentioned as being of "paramount importance to the welfare of the state."

November 9

2010—City Announces New Manager

On this day at 2:00 p.m. at city hall, Mayor Paul Fraim announced that Marcus Jones would be the new city manager. The forty-two-year-old Caroline County native had previous experience with the city, having been brought in as budget director in 2003 and promoted to assistant city director in 2007. In 2009, he filled a post in Richmond as budget and finance director. Reports said that he was hand selected and was the only candidate interviewed. Councilman Paul Riddick went on record as saying Jones was "the right guy for the job." Jones took over the position vacated by Regina V.K. Williams, who had held the post for twelve years.

November 10

1973—Routine Security Check Yields Fake Bills

What was described as a routine security check uncovered $45,000 in counterfeit money and the arrest of a twenty-one-year-old sailor aboard the USS *America*. The young man created the bogus bills in the *America*'s print shop. They were discovered when his brother came to retrieve the uncut cash, which was stashed in a briefcase. In addition to the counterfeit bills, the Secret Service also seized the plates that were used to print them. Officials described the money as "fair quality" and said it was printed on "bond paper with high rag content."

November 11

1959—Norfolk Man to Lead State Chamber Group

Curtis T. Brooks Jr. was elected to serve as president of the Virginia Association of Chamber of Commerce Executives. Brooks, who held the post of assistant executive manager of the Norfolk Chamber of Commerce, would be the twelfth president of the organization. He was chosen to lead the association at a meeting at Natural Bridge, Virginia. The slate of officers was completed by George A. Hillsman of Pulaski, Lois Millner of Franklin, Robert J. Johnson of Arlington and Frank Mantz of Portsmouth.

November 12

1985—Man to Serve Life Sentence for Spying

In Norfolk Federal Court, retired lieutenant commander Arthur Walker received three life sentences and was fined $250,000 for providing his brother, John A. Walker, with classified documents. The brothers, along with John's son Michael Walker and friend John A. Whitworth, were part of a spy ring that passed top-secret documents to Soviet authorities and was determined to be one of the most harmful in U.S. history. The sentencing judge, J. Calvett Clarke Jr., declared that Arthur Walker's "culpability was in his silence," referring to the fact that the fifty-one-year-old Walker knew of his brother's spying for years.

November 13

1922—Pilot Remains Unconscious at Public Health Hopsital

The day following an airplane crash in the Norfolk neighborhood of Lochaven, Lieutenant Colonel G.D. Chevalier remained unconscious at the Public Health Hospital on the Lafayette River near the site of the accident. Chevalier was a senior flight officer on the aircraft carrier *Langley*. At the time of his crash, he was flying from the Naval Base back to the *Langley*. Attending doctors predicted he would make a suitable recovery.

November 14

1883—Cotton Burns in Warehouse Fire

Four thousand bales of cotton waiting to be shipped to Boston aboard the steamer *Gaston* burned at the Norfolk and Western depot in a massive fire that also destroyed large quantities of lumber and miscellaneous freight. The blaze broke out in a Norfolk and Western warehouse and quickly spread to nearby buildings. The company's wharves were badly damaged in the blaze, and loads of freight were seen floating out with the tide. Tugboats along the waterfront aided in keeping the fire under control.

November 15

1920—Daniels Claims U.S. Naval Base to Be Best in World

Secretary of the Navy Josephus Daniels attended a breakfast meeting of the Norfolk and Portsmouth Rotarians. Following the morning meal, Daniels addressed the crowd. He shared his vision for Norfolk's naval base to be the greatest in the world and for the Norfolk Naval Yard in Portsmouth to be among the finest in the country. During his visit, Daniels toured both facilities, took part in an oyster roast at Cape Henry, kicked off a YMCA membership drive and addressed a citizens meeting at the Norfolk Armory Hall.

November 16

1981—Lady Monarchs Host Cuban National Team

As part of an eight-city tour of the United States, the Cuban national women's basketball team faced off against the two-time defending Association for Intercollegiate Athletics for Women champions, Old Dominion University's Lady Monarchs. Prior to the game at the ODU Field House, about fifty protesters demonstrated peacefully. Their contention was the presence of the Cuban team, whose home country they considered an active enemy of the United States. The Cuban women eked out a three-point victory, downing Old Dominion 71–68.

November 17

1909—Delegates Convene to Discuss Waterways

Three hundred delegates assembled at Norfolk for a meeting of the Atlantic Deeper Waterways Association. The convention was called to order by Pennsylvanian J. Hampton Moore, the group's president, who traveled to Norfolk from Philadelphia on the steamer *Lord Baltimore*, along with the other 217 northern delegates. The southern representatives were led by delegates Small and Thomas of North Carolina. Thomas spoke on the need to improve the country's coastline in order to fully benefit from the Panama Canal. Later in the week, President Taft and Mrs. Taft sailed down on the presidential yacht *Mayflower*, and the chief executive addressed the convention. The president and delegates then traveled to the Cape Henry Lighthouse for an oyster roast.

November 18

1900—French Ships Anchored Off Sewell's Point

Hundreds of people went on a Sunday outing and rode the Norfolk and Atlantic Terminal Railway to Sewells Point to see *La Cecille* and *La Suchet*, two French warships that were anchored a mile or so offshore. Upon arrival, rail passengers boarded the small steamer *Norfolk-of-the-Roads* that was owned by the railroad company and were ferried about the two French vessels in order to get a close-up look. An article in the *Virginian-Pilot* declared that while *La Cecille* would be "an ugly customer in battle, it is not as graceful as our American cruisers." While in town, the French ships loaded up with close to one thousand tons of coal.

November 19

1890—Real Estate Convention Convenes

A two-day meeting of Virginia real estate men—the first of its kind—was held in the city. Several committees were established, and plans were made for a follow-up meeting in Roanoke. While in town, guests were entertained in fine style and enjoyed many complimentary offerings such as trips around town and an oyster roast. Attendees were quick to praise their Norfolk hosts. One man from Petersburg claimed that Norfolk was the first place he had found where "his money was no good." Another attendee said he was "in love with Norfolk's way of doing things."

November 20

1899—German Steamer Olinda *On Fire, Heads for Norfolk*

The steel vessel *Olinda* sought refuge in Norfolk Harbor after catching fire off Cape Hatteras. It had departed New York for Cuba when fire caused the captain to display signals relaying the message "I am on fire." The German ship carried eighteen passengers in addition to its crew. After Captain Hansen displayed the message of distress, the *Olinda* was aided by the steamer *City of Washington* of the Ward Line. With great precariousness due to the frightful nature of an active sea, the passengers were transferred to the *City of Washington* and taken to Havana. When *Olinda* reached Norfolk, lightering vessels were sent to remove cargo.

November 21

2001—Garth Brooks Plays Welcome Concert Aboard USS Enterprise

Country pop star Garth Brooks performed aboard the aircraft carrier USS *Enterprise* eleven days after the vessel returned from a six-month deployment. Eight thousand complimentary tickets were distributed to crew members and families of the *Enterprise* and other Norfolk-based ships. Two thousand fans sat in bleacher seats while another six thousand fans watched from the floor. Brooks, whose father served as a U.S. marine, said he was thankful and respectful of the service of the men and women of the military. The concert, which also featured singer Jewel, was aired live on CBS. Brooks also performed a concert in Norfolk ten years earlier for veterans returning from the Persian Gulf War.

November 22

1935—Carnival Gal Kills Abusive Partner

Twenty-four-year-old carnival dancer Betty White found herself in Norfolk jail, held without bond after shooting William Williams, her common-law husband. The unfortunate incident unfolded in a Norfolk hotel room when Williams complained about cigarette smoke. White responded by blowing smoke in his face. Williams, who had a history of physically abusing the young blonde dancer, began to deliver blows to her head and chest. White then grabbed an automatic weapon and shot him in the back. When questioned about her feelings following the killing, the dancer responded, "I feel better than I felt in months, so help me God." At her trial, the jury ruled she acted in self-defense.

November 23

1814—Physician's Will to Educate Boys in Need

A prominent doctor penned his will in which he provided a sum of $3,000 to be held to draw interest that would be used for the support of less fortunate children in the city. Several boys were to be educated in "reading, writing and navigation" and to be bound to the commander of a warship or a merchant vessel. When the boys left school, new ones would take their places. This was Dr. Augustine Slaughter's way of assisting the country's young navy. Slaughter also made provisions for freeing and providing for his slaves.

November 24

1865—Baseball Match Pits Locals Against Soldiers

A number of citizens and local folk were on hand to view a baseball game between a local team, made up of nine players selected from the Juniper League, and a team formed from the Union Baseball Club of the Thirty-ninth Illinois Regiment that was stationed in the city. When the high-scoring two-hour game played "at the head of Cumberland Street" was over, the Midwesterners bested the Junipers forty-four runs to thirty. It was reported that the wind was a factor in the game and that the match was well played. After the final score was announced, the Junipers cheered the victors. The mood of the event was much enlivened by the Thirty-ninth Illinois Regiment Band.

November 25

2010—Jews and Christians Gather for Worship Tradition

On this morning, congregations from both Ohef Sholom Temple and Freemason Street Baptist Church met for a combined Thanksgiving service, a custom that started in 1927. Credit Emily LeBlanc Faber, who played the organ for both congregations. Instead of playing for two services on Thanksgiving Day, she suggested that both groups combine for one service. Each year, the service switches between Ohef Sholom and Freemason Street Baptist. Hymns are sung in English and Hebrew, and the visiting officiant gives the homily.

November 26

1899—Excursionists Travel to See Whale

A special "coaching party" was arranged to take day-trippers to view a much-publicized sixty-foot whale that had washed up at Pleasure Beach in Princess Ann County. The excursionists left at 10:30 a.m. from Trotters Drug Store at the corner of Main and Church Streets. The cost of round-trip passage was just one dollar. It was believed that the sea mammal was of the rorqual whale family, of which the humpback is a member, and that it was struck by a steamer, which caused its demise. Over the course of three or four weeks, thousands would make their way to see the sea creature.

November 27

1829—Council Passes Regulations for Loaf Bread

An ordinance was passed by the Common Council of the Borough of Norfolk regulating the production and sale of loaves of bread. It was required that loaves be made of "good and wholesome flour" and in four-pound, two-pound, one-pound and half-pound loaves. Those who produced bread from inferior flour or in sizes that did not comply with the ordinance would be subject to a five-dollar fine, and nonconforming loaves were subject to confiscation. The law was set to go into effect on January 1, 1830, but was repealed on December 22, 1829.

November 28

1954—House Collapse Kills Woman

A fifty-year-old woman died when the three-story building in which she lived "folded like an accordion." Firemen with searchlights found her body beneath the rubble a half hour after the building gave way. The woman, who was visiting with a friend at the time of the collapse, lived on the second floor, which became sandwiched between the first- and third-floor debris. The disaster, which came with no warning, took place on East Bute Street. The building was home to about thirty people.

November 29

1920—Grocers Hold Inaugural Meeting

The Retail Grocers' Association of Virginia met for their first annual convention. The two-day affair brought together grocers from Richmond,

Petersburg, Roanoke, Suffolk, Newport News and other cities in the state. The meeting was held in the Norfolk Chamber of Commerce offices with the city's own B.F. Morgan, president of the Grocers' Association, presiding. In addition to attending the Pure Food Show held by the Norfolk-Portsmouth Retail Grocers' Association, convention delegates viewed a program called "Modern Methods of Merchandising." A banquet, followed by an evening at the theater, completed the itinerary.

November 30

1999—Decker Brings Kitschy Identity to City

Norfolk lawyer Pete Decker suggested the idea of a citywide display of decorated mermaids, very much like the Cow Parade exhibit his wife, Bess, had just viewed on a jaunt to Chicago. Decker's plan was well received, and through a joint public and private venture, "Mermaids on Parade" turned out to be a very successful event. "Mermaid blanks," castings created by sculptor Kevin Gallup, were decorated by local artists and then "adopted" by businesses and interested parties who paid a $2,000 "fee." The colorful sculptures were then placed in front of public buildings, private companies and even people's homes. The mermaid then became a symbol of the city. Now Norfolk is sometimes referred to as the "Mermaid City."

DECEMBER

December 1

1907—Newspaper Calls Jamestown Exposition Failure

The day following the closing of the Jamestown Tercentennial Exposition, an event staged near Willoughby and designed to commemorate the 300th anniversary of the establishment of the Jamestown settlement, the *New York Times* published a lengthy article declaring the event a failure. The exposition, which took place between April and November, racked up a substantial amount of debt, and transportation was described as "miserable." The administration and management of the exposition was led by a board of governors beset with "turmoil and strife." Attendance was lower than expected. On good days, fifty thousand people visited the exposition, but those days were few and far between. A highlight was North Carolina Day, when sixty thousand people toured the exposition.

December 2

1941—Services Held for Philanthropist and Former Mayor

Funeral services were held at Christ and St. Luke's Episcopal Church for Fergus Reid, who died days earlier at Norfolk General Hospital following a lengthy illness. Reid, who came to the city in 1891, made his living as a cotton merchant and as such was a member of the New York Cotton Exchange and the Liverpool Cotton Association. Norfolk General Hospital, the Norfolk Community Fund and Sweet Briar College near Lynchburg, Virginia, were recipients of Reid's generosity.

December 3

1953—Chaplain Flown to Bermuda for Chanukah

The Jewish Welfare Board announced that David Hachen, the Jewish chaplain at the Norfolk Naval Training Station, had been flown to Bermuda, where President Eisenhower, British prime minister Winston Churchill and French premier Joseph Laniel were in the throes of their "Big Three" Conference. Hachen would perform Chanukah services for Jewish military and civilian personnel from the United States, Great Britain and France. The Jewish Welfare Board sent menorahs, candles and dreidels. The Chanukah service was held in the in the U.S. Naval Chapel at Naval Air Station Bermuda.

December 4

1920—President-Elect Receives Warm Welcome

A tanned president-elect and Mrs. Warren G. Harding arrived at Newport News aboard the steamship *Pastores* following a trip to the Panama Canal Zone. The scene was one of much fanfare as seaplanes flew and dipped overhead and dirigibles floated over Hampton Roads. Ships from various countries were decorated in their national colors. After stops and speeches on the peninsula, Harding arrived in Norfolk and viewed a drill of ten thousand sailors and addressed the crowd from the reviewing stand. In the evening, he spoke to a group of eight thousand at the Billy Sunday Tabernacle. Bolstering America's maritime trade and fostering global relationships were the subjects of his many short speeches during his stay.

December 5

1872—Norfolk Pears Spotlighted in Article

The periodical *California Farmer and Journal of Useful Sciences* reprinted an article from the *New York Horticulturalist*, which sang the praises of pears grown in Norfolk and its environs. It was noted that pears raised in Norfolk were cultivated on large tracts ranging from 50 to 160 acres.

Pears harvested from local orchards fetched between seven and nine dollars a bushel in New York City. Those owning orchards were Mr. Whitehead, with 5,200 trees, and Mr. Weir with a slightly smaller orchard. Mr. Leighton had 7,000 trees.

December 6

1952—Fish Bowl Festivities

Colorful floats, majorettes, dressed-up automobiles, Boy Scouts and marching units paraded their way from Carver Park to Meyers Field as a prelude to the Annual Fish Bowl Classic football game. Marching bands from I.C. Norcom, Booker T. Washington, Jacox School and the Norfolk Division of Virginia State Teacher's College warmed up the crowd prior to the battle on the gridiron between the Norfolk Division and Elizabeth City State Teacher's College from Elizabeth City, North Carolina. The Fish Bowl was sponsored by the Nobles of Arabia Temple #12 of the Mystic Shrine. Elizabeth City eked out a 6–2 victory.

December 7

2006—Sweet Pea to Enter Boxing Hall of Fame

Norfolk's Pernell "Sweet Pea" Whitaker was voted into the International Boxing Hall of Fame. Ballots were cast by boxing historians from around the globe and representatives from the Boxing Writers Association. Whitaker was voted in on his first round of eligibility, along with Panamanian fighter Roberto Duran. Sweet Pea won more than two hundred amateur bouts before clenching a gold medal in the 1984 Olympics in Los Angeles, California. He turned pro the same year and during his career won titles in four weight classes. *Ring Magazine* named Whitaker 1989 Fighter of the Year.

December 8

1894—Grand Banquet Held to Honor International Trade

An assemblage of worthy patrons representing "businessmen, capitalists and editors" made its way to the Hygeia Hotel at Old Point Comfort to celebrate the arrival of the *Lamberts Point*, the first ship of the Norfolk and North American Line, which would usher in a new line of trade between the city and Liverpool. The shipping line was created to export goods of the Norfolk and Western Railroad terminal at Lamberts Point. On its first trip eastward, the *Lamberts Point* was laden with 64,000 bushels of grain taken on at Newport News, 9,000 bushels taken on at the Norfolk and Western grain elevator in Norfolk and 7,500 bales of cotton loaded at Lamberts Point. The ship was described as a "model vessel" and "alone on the modern cargo carriers."

December 9

1859—Son of Publisher Feared Murdered

Eleven-year-old Virginius Leonard, son of Abram F. Leonard, the editor of the *Norfolk Argus*, was found dead at the National Hotel with a fatal wound in his neck. It was believed that the boy had been murdered, which caused much angst and distress in the city. Following an investigation by the coroner, it was determined that young Virginius, who was described as bright and promising, accidently shot himself.

December 10

2008—Hearing Held on Bridge Tunnel Expansion

Two hundred citizens, including elected officials from across Hampton Roads, turned out at the Granby High School Auditorium to voice their views on six different plans to expand the Hampton Roads Bridge Tunnel, the important route between Ocean View and Hampton. Norfolk officials were against any plans to expand, saying that it would bring down the quality of life to those living in Ocean View and Willoughby. Mayor Paul

Fraim drew applause when he said there were "grave concerns about all these alternatives." He believed the best solution was a third crossing option connecting Norfolk with the Monitor-Merrimac Tunnel.

December 11

1951—Redevelopment Begins in Norfolk and in the Nation

Two thousand people, including members of the national media, descended on the city to witness the start of the first redevelopment project in the nation financed mostly by the 1949 Federal Housing Act. The demolition of a slum building at 755 Smith Street downtown was the first of many substandard structures to be removed. New public housing projects such as Young Park, Diggs Park, Grandy Village and Roberts Park were built to offer families more modern and updated habitations. New municipal buildings and wider streets downtown were built as part of the new Norfolk. Critics claim the city tore down too much too fast.

December 12

1914—Supplies Arrive for Belgian Relief

Communities across Virginia were collecting clothing and other necessities to send to war-ravaged Belgium, which was suffering at the hands of a German invasion. Relief Fund headquarters was in Norfolk, where supplies were sent. Loading of the vessel *Lynorta*, with a capacity of six thousand tons, began at the end of December. The ship, loaded "to the hatches," departed in January to carry the relief supplies from the Old Dominion. In addition to donations of clothing, monetary gifts from across the state were coming in. Flour was in high demand. Colonel Henry L. Boykin, who served as chairman of the State Relief Commission, oversaw the collection of goods.

December 13

1959—Chapel Dedicated, Named for Levy

The navy's first permanent Jewish Chapel was dedicated in honor of Uriah Phillips Levy (1792–1862), the navy's first Jewish flag officer, who was known for his opposition to the flogging of sailors. Joshua L. Goldberg acted as officiant of the service that was described as a display of "religious unity in the armed forces." The Norfolk Jewish Community Council and National Jewish Welfare Board sponsored the ceremony along with the navy. Levy and his descendants can also be credited with preserving Monticello, which he purchased in 1823.

December 14

1999—Council Considers Public Election of Mayor

On this day, Norfolk City Council members voted to petition the Virginia General Assembly for a charter change. It would then be possible to conduct a public referendum to determine if there was public sentiment behind popular election of Norfolk's mayor instead of council members selecting the candidate for the office. In 2006, Norfolk's mayor was directly elected by citizens.

December 15

1932—Food Prices in City Drop Dramatically

For the monthly reporting period between November 15 and December 15, food prices in Norfolk dropped 4 percent, one of the most noticeable declines among the nation's large cities, according to the United States Labor Department. In Virginia's capital of Richmond, food prices dropped just 1 percent. The only other city in the nation with a larger drop in food prices was Chicago. For the monthly reporting period, the Windy City could boast a 5 percent drop in food prices.

December 16

1900—Sloop Ashore, Sails Still Set

Two men set out in a rowboat to investigate a beached schooner between Lamberts Point and Sewells Point. It was determined that the vessel was the *Sam Seed* of Portsmouth. The boat's mainsail was set, and its jib had been torn by the wind. There was no one aboard when it was boarded. The ship's papers were in order and listed the master as Ira Cahoon, who had recently set sail from Newport News. His wife offered a reward for information about Cahoon's disappearance or return of his body. It was believed Captain Cahoon was knocked overboard by the ship's boom. He was described as five feet seven inches with graying whiskers and missing three teeth in his lower jaw.

December 17

1903—Telegraph Operator Leaks Wright Story

Jim Gray, a telegraph operator in Norfolk, received a message from the Kitty Hawk Weather Station to be sent to Bishop Milton Wright in Dayton, Ohio. The message was intended for the father of Orville and Wilbur Wright, and it included news of the brothers' four successful flights that day. Gray telegraphed Kitty Hawk and asked to share the story with the local paper, but the highly private Wrights declined. Gray, however, went ahead and contacted some fellows at the *Virginian-Pilot*. The three of them cobbled a story around the facts they had. The following day, readers of the *Pilot* were greeted with the attention-grabbing, although hyperbolic headline, "Flying Machine Soars 3 Miles in Teeth of High Wind over Sand Hills and Waves at Kitty Hawk on Carolina Coast."

December 18

1922—Norfolk Prepares for "Dry" Christmas

Federal and state prohibition officials, along with Norfolk and county police forces, ramped up efforts to keep any "booze yachts" from coming to Norfolk from the West Indies. The federal officials, known as revenuers, were also planning to raid any supply ships already at sea. Raids were also planned on the illegal stills in neighboring rural Princess Anne and Norfolk Counties that manufactured moonshine or corn liquor. This was the first Christmas holiday since the state prohibition law had gone into effect on November 1.

December 19

1972—Rembrandt Pledged to Museum

Automobile industry heir Walter P. Chrysler Jr. announced his plans to give the Rembrant painting *Samson Threatening His Father in Law* to the Chrysler Museum. The work of art was valued between $1 and $3 million. Court approval of Chrysler's donation of his art collection to the city was a condition upon which the deal hinged. If the donation was court-approved, Chrysler would, over a period of years, donate between two hundred and four hundred works of art that were currently on loan to the museum. The museum's board of directors had been at odds with the facility's benefactor because of his exchanging of paintings in and out of the collection.

December 20

1897—Trial Begins for Olive Pecker *Mutaineer*

The trial of John Anderson, cook aboard the schooner *Olive Pecker*, began in Norfolk Federal Court. Anderson was accused of killing mate William Wallace Saunders by shooting him four times. The ship was bound for South America from Boston with a cargo of lumber. Shipmates testified that Anderson shot both the captain and the mate after Captain Whitman scolded Anderson for pouring water on his dog. After the shootings, Anderson summonsed the crew and had them throw the bodies overboard and set the *Olive Pecker* afire. The crew then made for land in smaller vessels. Anderson was found guilty, and he appealed the decision all the way to the U.S. Supreme Court. He was executed in Norfolk during a gruesome spectacle. He fell to the cobblestones and survived after the hanging rope broke but was strung up a second time and hung again.

December 21

1944—Article Spotlights Navy Wives' Effort

A syndicated story ran in the *Danville Bee* on this day (and in other newspapers during the week) that spotlighted the work of Mrs. George Seitz, who recruited seventy Norfolk navy wives to serve as bus and trolley drivers to move defense workers to and from work and to allow sailors on liberty a chance to travel off base. Seitz was picked for the task while taking a course at William and Mary, and as the wife of a commodore at the base, she knew of the benefits that increased transit opportunities would bring. A female-friendly employee lounge with showers, where drivers could stay after a late-night shift, helped the ladies feel comfortable.

December 22

1885—Norfolkian Represents in Oyster Contest

In an incredible contest, Frank Barrett opened 2,500 oysters in just under two hours and twenty-four minutes. Barrett was described as "short and stout," wearing rubber boots and a black cap and appearing as a "typical oyster opener." Known as the sculler, his method of shucking involved hitting the shell with a hammer and then inserting a knife between the shells. His chief opponent, John Gillen of New York, used just a Long Island oyster knife. The scene was described as having shells and oysters flying through the air. In the close contest, Barrett was done a disservice when a fresh batch of oysters was laid upon his pile of shells. The men were clocked each time they shucked 500 bivalves.

December 23

1919—Steamer Madison *Aground Near Craney Island*

Around 8:00 p.m. on this day, the steamer *Madison* of the Old Dominion Line ran aground on a mud flat on the southeast side of Craney Island in Norfolk Harbor. It was carrying eighty-two passengers and was headed to New York City. Tugboats were immediately sent to aid the stranded vessel, and it was believed that the steamer would float off the soft mud at the next high tide. There were no attempts made to remove the passengers. Heavy fog was the reason for the grounding.

December 24

1999—Vet Finds Home for Beloved Lab-Mix, a Christmas Story

A seventy-two-year-old veteran who was moving to a Veterans Administration hospital in Tennessee because of cancer shared news at a Christmas Eve press conference at the El Dorado Court trailer park. He found a suitable caretaker for his dog Cruiser. After Reece Appleton offered his $2,500 trailer for someone to live in and take care of his mixed breed dog, he received over 250 responses from people across the country. A former neighbor, Bo Matthews, agreed to adopt Cruiser. Matthews, who knew Appleton, said neighbors referred to him as Sarge. The owner and the manager of El Dorado Court were instrumental in the positive outcome of the story.

December 25

1946—Granby Comets Represent in Miami

The Granby High School Comet football team was handed its first loss following thirty-two wins in a row. The match, held at Miami's Orange Bowl, was the North-South game, and the victors were the Classical Eleven from Lynn, Massachusetts' Classical High School. Over eighteen thousand fans were on hand to watch the close matchup that was a benefit for Shriner's Mahi Shrine Temple. The final score of the game was 21–14.

December 26

1899—Miss Moore Fêtes Sister's Twelfth Birthday

In order to mark the milestone of her sister's birthday, Miss Emma Moore entertained a dozen or so young people. Miss Mary Moore was turning twelve years old. The event included music and recitations, cake walks and a song presented by Miss Mamie Thomas, accompanied by Miss Myrtle Titus. Music was kindly provided by Professor Ed Shuster, who played piano. Refreshments were served at 11:00 p.m., after which the young people "dispersed."

December 27

1865—City Masons Hold Grand Ball

The Masonic Order of Norfolk, Atlantic Lodge No. 2 threw a grand ball at Glenn Theater, which was finely decorated for the dance. A supper was served that featured oysters, roast goose and Polish salad (consumed by the sensible folk), while those with a "poetic temperament" partook of a confection called a Baltimore Kiss. Dancing began at 10:30 p.m. and opened with a quadrille, danced by thirty-two couples. This was followed by waltzes, polkas, a mazurka (a lively Polish dance in triple meter), a redowa (a Czech dance featuring leaping waltz steps) and, of course, the Virginia Reel. Beautiful women from both Norfolk and Portsmouth were "bewitching," and they were joined by lovely ladies from Baltimore and Richmond. The ball was held on the death date of St. John the Evangelist.

December 28

1981—Country's First Test Tube Baby Born

Weighing just five pounds, two ounces, Elizabeth Jordan Carr was born at 7:46 a.m. at Norfolk General Hospital. She was the first child in the United States not conceived by traditional means but rather by in vitro fertilization (IVF). Fourteen children in the United Kingdom and Australia were born following IVF procedures, prior to Elizabeth's birth. Under the careful eyes of Drs. Howard and Georgeanna Jones, who opened an IVF clinic at Eastern Virginia Medical School, mother Judy Carr, whose identity was kept secret during her pregnancy, successfully carried the baby, who was delivered by obstetrician Dr. Mason Andrews.

December 29

1955—Embezzling Spinster Goes to Jail

Miss Minnie Mangum, a sixty-year-old spinster described as a pudgy yet generous woman who wore sensible shoes, on this day was taken to jail by two Norfolk detectives. During her tenure as an employee of the Commonwealth Saving and Loan, she embezzled nearly $3 million. In short, Miss Minnie was sort of a modern-day Robin Hood. She used the diverted funds to finance projects and businesses that she felt worthy. Some of the money went to family and friends. The author of this book believes that Miss Minnie might've backed businesses on North Carolina's Outer Banks.

December 30

1806—Ordinance Provides for Surveyor

The Common Council of the Borough of Norfolk passed an act that allowed for a mathematical surveyor, determined his duties and provided for his salary and any associated fees. The surveys performed by the borough surveyor would be as valid as surveys performed by any county surveyor. The act also provided for the procurement of a theodolite and other instruments needed to perform surveys. One of the first duties of the surveyor would be to create a complete plan or map of the borough under the direction of the mayor, recorder and aldermen.

December 31

1899—Busy Steamer Decorated for Holidays

Trains from the city to Ocean View carried a number of passengers who then boarded the steamer *Ocean View* for the trip between Willoughby Spit and Old Point Comfort. Excursionists were headed to spend New Year's Eve at the Chamberlain or Hygeia Hotel. It was noted that the *Ocean View* "presented a pretty scene," decorated for Christmas with holly and mistletoe. George W. Mansfield, the vessel's captain; E.F. Wheeler, mate; and Thomas W. Howard, purser, all played a role in the *Ocean View*'s decoration. Passengers were complimentary of both the decorations and the superior service and attention they were afforded.

SELECTED BIBLIOGRAPHY

Borum, Samuel R., with the Norfolk Chamber of Commerce. *Norfolk, Va., Port and City. Facts and Figures of Its Trade, Commerce and Manufactures*. Norfolk, VA: Norfolk Chamber of Commerce, 1896.

Bryant, James K. *The 36th Infantry United States Colored Troops in the Civil War: A History and Roster*. Jefferson, NC: McFarland & Co, 2012.

Burton, H.W. *The History of Norfolk, Virginia*. Norfolk, VA: Norfolk Virginian, 1877.

Butler, Stuart L. "Defending Norfolk: An Early Battle with the British in 1813 Saves a Thriving American Port." *Prologue Magazine* (Spring 2013).

Cohodas, Nadine. *Queen: The Life and Music of Dinah Washington*. New York: Pantheon Books, 2004.

Leidholdt, Alexander S. "Lenoir Chambers (1891–1970)." *Encyclopedia Virginia*. A publication of the Virginia Foundation for the Humanities. http://encyclopediavirginia.org/Chambers_Joseph_Lenoir_Jr_1891-1970 (accessed April 6, 2014).

Leidholdt, A.S. "Louis I. Jaffé (ca. 1888–1950)." *Encyclopedia Virginia*. A publication of the Virginia Foundation for the Humanities. March 23, 2014. http://www.EncyclopediaVirginia.org/Jaffé_Louis_Isaac_ca_1888-1950. (accessed October 5, 2014).

Marshall, Alex. "Urban Renewal in Norfolk." http://www.alexmarshall.org/2007/09/24/urban-renewal-in-norfolk.

McPhillips, Peggy. "Joseph A. Jordan Jr.—Civil Rights Pioneer." Norfolk Public Library Celebrates Black History Month, February 2014.

Norfolk, Virginia Industrial Commission. *Norfolk, Virginia: "The Sunrise City by the Sea."* Norfolk, VA: Burke & Gregory, 1914.

Norfolk, Virginia Police Division. *Norfolk Police Department: Into Our Third Century of Service, 1797–2003.* Paducah, KY: Turner Publishing Company, 2003.

Ordinances of the Borough of Norfolk Passed Since 1829. Norfolk, VA: T.G. Broughton, 1840.

Shampoe, Clay, and Thomas R. Garrett. *Baseball in Norfolk, Virginia.* Charleston, SC: Arcadia, 2003.

Taylor, Michael V., and Gordon B. Calhoun. "Naval Station Norfolk." *Encyclopedia Virginia.* A publication of the Virginia Foundation for the Humanities. September 19, 2012. http://www.encyclopediavirginia.org/Naval_Station_Norfolk (accessed August 23, 2014).

Treadway, Sandra G. "Sarah Lee Fain (1888–1962)." *Encyclopedia Virginia.* A publication of the Virginia Foundation for the Humanities. April 7, 2011. http://www.encyclopediavirginia.org/Fain_Sarah_Lee_1888-1962 (accessed March 9, 2014).

Virginia Medical Semi-Monthly 2, no. 22, (January 28, 1898).

"Weddings of the Year." *People,* July 24, 1995.

Wertenbaker, Thomas Jefferson. *Norfolk: Historic Southern Port. Edited by Marvin W. Schlegel.* Durham, NC: Duke University Press, 1962.

Yarsinske, Amy Waters. *Ocean View.* Dover, NH: Arcadia, 1998.

Newspapers

Ames (IA) Daily Tribune
Boston Evening Transcript
California Farmer and Journal of Useful Sciences
Centralia (Washington) Daily Chronicle
Charleston (WV) Gazette Mail
Danville (VA) Bee
Danville (VA) Register
Elizabeth City (NC) State Teacher's College News Letter
Farmington (NM) Daily Times
Frederick (MD) News-Post
Fredericksburg (VA) Star
Harrisonburg (VA) Daily News Record
Middleton (NY) Times
New York Times
Norfolk (VA) Post
Norfolk Virginian
Pacific Stars and Stripes
Paris (TX) News
Petersburg (VA) Progress Index
Pulaski (VA) Southwest Times
Richmond (VA) Jewish South
Richmond (VA) Times Dispatch
Sacramento (CA) Daily Union
San Francisco Call
Statesville (NC) Record and Landmark
Titusville (PA) Herald
USA Today
Washington (DC) Afro-American
Washington Post
Winchester (VA) Star

ABOUT THE AUTHOR

Sarah Downing was born on a cold snowy night in Norfolk, Virginia, a fate secured because of her grandfathers. One was career navy, and the other came to serve as chief of police in the 1950s.

Following graduation from high school in Maryland (way back in the 1980s), Downing moved to North Carolina's Outer Banks to be near the seashore and closer to her grandparents. After working at the Outer Banks History Center for a number of years, she began to write local history books with The History Press.

In 2015, Sarah transferred to the Western Regional Archives in Asheville. She is enjoying the mountain air and exploring her new surroundings and all the fascinating places in Western North Carolina.

Visit us at
www.historypress.net

This title is also available as an e-book